The Church and Urban Power Structure

CHRISTIAN PERSPECTIVES
ON SOCIAL PROBLEMS

Gayraud S. Wilmore, *General Editor*

The Church and Urban Power Structure

by

GEORGE D. YOUNGER

Philadelphia

THE WESTMINSTER PRESS

LIBRARY OF CONGRESS CATALOG CARD No. 63–9774

PUBLISHED BY THE WESTMINSTER PRESS ®
PHILADELPHIA 7, PENNSYLVANIA

PRINTED IN THE UNITED STATES OF AMERICA

Contents

Foreword

THIS BOOK IS ONE OF SEVERAL TO APPEAR DURING THE next few years in a series entitled Christian Perspectives on Social Problems. This is an attempt to meet a challenge from an exceedingly robust minority of laymen for brief, readable analyses of cultural problems from a theological perspective. It is intended to help them *think theologically* about some of the exasperatingly difficult problems of society, both the issues relating to life in America and those linking this nation to the destiny of the world.

Recent researches on family life have found laymen obsessed with "loving, happy relations" in the family, with child-rearing and personal problems of status and adjustment, but with little comprehension of how private troubles bisect public issues. This curious fascination with selfhood to the neglect of neighborhood is not, however, a universal malaise of Protestantism. A minority, perhaps, but a minority that refuses to be lightly regarded by ecclesiastical officialdom, is demanding to know the meaning of events of our day for the Christian faith and to demonstrate the critical and renewing power of faith in secular society.

It is to these doughty men and women that the several volumes of the Christian Perspectives on Social Problems series are directed, and it is hoped that they not only will

1

make for an unsettling reading experience but will provide stimulating material for small-group study and discussion. To that end, questions for discussion are appended to each of the books as starters for fruitful controversy.

No series on social problems could overlook the fact that 112 million Americans reside in 212 metropolitan areas. A new situation has been given to the church and to the society. It is characterized by the elaboration, physically, socially, and politically, of the metropolitan complex, with its tremendous impact upon the personality and style of life of most Americans.

Christian laymen have needed, and have now in this volume, a Biblical and theological examination of this "new situation" that takes with utmost seriousness the fact that the instrumentality by which it is ordered or disordered is *power*. George D. Younger, minister of the Mariners' Temple Baptist Church on New York City's East Side, demonstrates in these pages that power also can be a servant of God. The prerequisite is to learn how it is structured in the city and what the church can do about it.

Clearly, this is not just another book bemoaning the plight of the urban church in the asphalt jungle. We have had quite enough of that! The focus is rather upon the context of power in which, for good or ill, things and people are dynamically interrelated in Metropolis. The conclusion is that the church, "abounding in hope," can and must share in the continuing reconstruction of metropolitan life.

GAYRAUD S. WILMORE

Pittsburgh, Pennsylvania

Chapter I

Who Decides?

AS WE VIEW OUR AMERICAN CITIES FROM AN AIR-plane as it circles before making a landing, the most strik-ing things about them are the buildings and the pattern they make on the landscape. Taller buildings at the center mark the hub of business and government; then the neighborhoods spread out from the center in a variety of patterns, depending on the way in which rivers, hills, highways, railroads, and other arteries move out from the heart; then the suburbs and outlying parts reach to the horizon—and beyond it in the larger metropolitan areas. Finally, scattered over the entire area are the places of commerce and industry, most noticeable at night when the winking neon signs and gaudy lights share with the blue-lit factory windows and smoky glare in creating is-lands and belts that lie anywhere from close at the center to the outer reaches. A vast concentration of buildings and people—that is what a city is, we say to ourselves.

Each city makes a different pattern on the landscape, showing that it has had a different history and has had to face different obstacles, natural and man-made. New York, the home of the United Nations, thrusts its proud skyscrapers up into the sky from foundations drilled deep

3

into the solid rock of its central island. Chicago, agent for the Middle West, sends its railroad spokes north and west and south from its lakeshore site. Denver marches its neat checkerboards toward the Rockies on one side and the prairie on the other. San Francisco perches on its hills overlooking the bay. And Los Angeles, with all its related communities, sprawls over the canyons and valleys that surround its downtown offices. The sight of the city's buildings from the air can awaken in the homebound traveler or the visiting tourist that same shock of recognition that once was reserved for mountains and rivers and valleys. Buildings seem to make the city.

Yet we are misled if we assume that the substance of a city is its buildings. Cut off from the supply of fuel and power, food and water, or denied communication with the surrounding area and a steady flow of new population, our American cities would shrivel and die, leaving their buildings behind as majestic proof that men once lived in this way, like buried Pompeii or the shrines of Angkor Wat or the pyramids of Chichén Itzá.

A city is primarily a social organism, a way of living together. The buildings and streets may be the shell within which this hermit crab society finds shelter, but the life of that society is in its people. All that can be seen from the air is the pattern these people and their predecessors have made upon the landscape. If we are to know the city as it is, we must walk its streets and meet its citizens.

THE CITY SEEN FROM THE GROUND

Viewed from its sidewalks and streets, the city seems to be a million things at once. The swiftly moving crowds that ebb and flow through the downtown areas may first impress us by their numbers, but as we look closer we are struck even more by their diversity. Like snowflakes viewed through a pocket glass, each is different from the others. The people we pass seem endless in their variety, though sharing a common humanity. And every detail of the scene around them—buildings, streets, signs, lights, objects in store windows, the very litter in the gutter—shares the same multiplicity. Even when the earth is opened up beneath the pavement or in a vacant lot, the network of pipes and wires or the ruins of old foundations and scattered debris have the same overpowering variety.

Yet, unlike the diversity of life to be found in a drop of swamp water or the thousand creeping, crawling things to be seen on the forest floor, this variety is almost completely the result of man's conscious effort. It may ultimately be held in being by the sovereign will of Almighty God, but its more immediate cause is the will of some man or group of men. Why does the sidewalk change here from cement to slabs of broken slate? Why can that building shoot into the air with a perpendicular front when another must go up in terraced setbacks like some latter-day ziggurat? Why are the streetlights so close together in this part of town, when they seem so dim and far apart over on the other side? The answers to these and any of the millions of other questions that could be asked about the city as we see it from the ground are to be found, not in the mind and will of God, but in the mind and will of men.

Many times the very reason for a particular law or rule or structure or custom or sign has been lost in the records of past years or buried with the men who brought it into being. Now it is shielded from examination and change by the forces of habit and clerkdom which guarantee that what is shall be—unless another act of man secures an alternative. Thus, much of what we see from the ground has begun to achieve a being of its own.

In other cases, the reasons do not lie above the surface for every eye to see. But a check into the deeds office can reveal who holds title and sway over the land on which we walk. And a look at the docket in the courts can show who are the protagonists and antagonists. And an act of challenge to the state of things as they are can often bring us face to face with those whose interest it is to keep them that way. This society of the city has its movers and its shakers; it has its human causes from whose heads and hands flow the results we see on every side.

The City Seen from the Outside

A steady diet of newspaper headlines and feature stories can begin to give the regular reader an impression that he really knows what makes the city move. The press is always ready to place in the public record the names and statements of those who are popularly presumed to be making the decisions. The mayor seems to be on the front page almost every day. The chamber of commerce and the labor unions, the leading politicians and the heads of various welfare organizations, the local Roman Catholic archbishop and an occasional Protestant leader—these are some of the main actors in the drama that is placed in people's hands every day to be read on the way to work or in the living room before supper.

"Mayor Refuses Wage Hike to Sanitation Drivers." "Business Groups Call for More Downtown Parking." "Bricklayers' Walkout Ties Up Construction." "Mulloy Charges Jones with Doubletalk." "Jones Questions Mulloy's Record." And so it goes, round and round in a never-ending succession of cause and effect. The avid reader feels that, once he knows the cast of characters and the special terminology they use, he is getting an inside view of the basic decisions about his life and the life of all who live in his city.

Yet this is an illusory sense of immediacy and involvement. He is about as close to the decision makers and the basic decisions as the television fan watching his favorite character play the part of a medical doctor is close to the day-to-day life and decisions of his local hospital. He can sense the gross outlines of what is going on and acquire some of the basic vocabulary. However, he is still far away from the actual place where decisions are made and the multiplicity of causes that must be taken into account.

At times the person who is trying to keep "informed" on the progress of civic affairs through the information available to him in the press is actually misled concerning the true nature of the life of his city. Although the mayor may make many appearances and speeches in the course of a week and be quoted in the newspapers as the source of government policy, most of the actual decisions are made not by the chief executive officer but by his associates and the many officials, large and small, who constitute the city administration. Although "business" and "labor" are handy labels for the reader as he skims over headlines, each covers such a wide range of attitudes and policies that it proves to be an abstraction signifying almost nothing when it is applied to the men in business suits who sit down for collective bargaining. And the ebb and flow of personal political drama, the cops-and-robbers theme supplied by crime, the annual succession of civic observances, festivals, campaigns and fund drives, the tides of popular interests and fads—all these may be "news," yet none points directly to the people who have the most to say about the life of the city.

THE CITY SEEN FROM THE INSIDE

When one gets inside the social structure of a city, he begins to understand that the basic policies and the most important decisions are made by a relatively small group of people. This observation is borne out by the results of study by trained social observers. They find that, although

a large number of people work at the job of executing
policy at lower levels and different groups interest themselves in different areas of city life, the basic decisions
at the policy-making level are made by a very few people.

Call them the "power elite," "top leadership," or what
you will, these few leaders are not only the decision
makers according to reputation. Study of the processes
by which key decisions are made shows also that they set
the basic framework within which all other decisions are
made. Wealth, educational background, prestige, fame,
involvement in civic organizations, and membership in
social clubs all help to reinforce the essential power which
this limited group possesses by virtue of its position in the
life of the city. Obviously, no one in this group possesses
absolute power; yet power over basic decisions and ar-
rangements is theirs.

Those who have studied the subject are clear in indi-
cating that the two areas in which most of these top
leaders are to be found are the world of business and the
world of government and politics. Education, organized
labor, the professions, civic associations, welfare organizations, cultural groups, religious institutions—all play their
share in the city's life. But the prime movers are to be
found in business and politics.

One observer has made it plain that no city has a "Mr.
Big," who calls the shots for every part of its life. That
sort of picture may be adequate in a half-hour television
mystery or a Superman comic strip, but it does not do
justice to the greater complexity of a real city's life. Yet
in every city there is a small group, concentrated in the
fields of business and government, and shifting in membership as the generations come and go, that concerns itself with the city's "welfare" as seen from the broad perspective of its penthouse apartments or rooftop office
suites or suburban estates.

This group of civic leaders, however, is often difficult to identify. Many are hardly known to the average newspaper reader, whereas others appear on the front page day after day. Some stick close to the narrow routine of finance, real estate, commerce, or their city department, while others are broad in their interests and become involved on every side. Yet, it is in precisely this sort of amorphous group, sometimes hardly conscious of its own power and operating more on the level of personal relations than of organized strength, that decisions are made which have consequences that reach down to the tiniest child and the humblest household in the wide metropolitan area.

By their ability to loosen the treasuries of private investment or government budgets, by their ability to get hostile, contradictory interests to move forward in a common direction once that direction has been set, by their ability to drag their feet or work against proposals for civic change, these leaders shape the outlines of the city's life. All other leaders must operate within the framework outlined by this group. All other attempts to work out a vision of civic life must ultimately be judged in terms of the financial and political criteria that this group brings to its consideration of all problems. "What's good for business," "What's good for the party," "What's good for the city"—all become interchangeable statements at the top level of leadership.

THE CITY SEEN FROM UNDERNEATH

Contradictory as it may seem, the result of this concentration of the power of ultimate decision in the hands of a very few in the American city is not to create a vast monolithic pyramid with a small privileged group sitting astride a larger corps of underlings who ride herd on the vast mass underneath. Such has been the pattern of many societies of ancient times and could be the result if this system were more carefully planned and rationally organized. But the genius of American society has been its pluralism, its willingness to allow contradictions to exist, its tolerance for competing ideologies and ways of life, its ability to combine energy and inertia.

Although we can speak in a general way of a small core of leadership concentrated in the spheres of business and government, the organization of the life of our cities more nearly resembles a set of pyramids than one great unified structure. Each pyramid—be it business, government, labor, the professions, education, civic affairs, welfare, the arts, or religion—has its own structure, its own leaders, its own goals and accepted patterns of behavior, and its own public to which it appeals for support. On any given issue facing the body politic, these structures move in response to their own understanding of the problem at hand —yet always within the wider framework set by the policies of business and government leaders. Little wonder that some analysts can speak of this as an environment (ecology) of games—each with its own rules!

However, to the average resident of the metropolitan area, feeling only the impact of the decisions made at the top levels and the countless stratagems being tried out in the various pyramids of city life in between, there is little awareness of what really creates the conditions of his life. The tendency of the average city dweller to speak of "them" and to believe that most of the issues of life are beyond his control is not a paranoid delusion; it has real basis in the facts of his situation. A majority of the decisions that affect his life most deeply are made outside the neighborhood in which he lives—in a Washington office or on the floor of the state legislature or at a businessmen's lunch downtown or in the program department of a television chain or in the cubbyholes of bureaucracy that determine and carry out policy in education, health, welfare, housing, labor, employment, traffic, street lighting, sanitation, and a hundred other issues of life-and-death importance. Someone in authority, whether consciously or unconsciously, is squeezing ever tighter the limits within which destiny may be sought and fulfilled.

In none of these areas is the control securely lodged with any one group of people, nor are its terms securely fixed. The clash of personal, organizational, and group interest is a constant struggle for control over a part of the area of decision or the terms of the decision to be made on a given issue. All the estates of modern urban society—all the pyramids of power, each playing its own game—have entered this conflict. And control of the power to decide often becomes more crucial than the content of the decisions.

At a more local level the city dweller can begin to see dimly the outlines of this conflict. The wider struggle for control has its skirmishes, its battles, and its periods of occupation that are fought out in the arena of the neighborhood or district where people live or work. The boss, the shop steward, the local politician, the lesser officials such as police captains, school principals, health officers, and all manner of inspectors and administrators, the newer quasi-officials such as the "social engineers" (community organizers, sociologists, social workers, and the like), and even the local clergy are all engaged in a grotesque ballet that responds far more precisely to the rhythm of the larger struggle for control than to the cries and dumb anxieties of those among whom their work is set.

Seen from underneath, the life of the city as a social organism becomes a contradictory pattern of conflict and struggle among remote powers that seldom seem to reflect the deepest problems and desires of the city's residents. They are reduced to "making a living" or "trying to get along" and feel little sense of participation or need to share in shaping the conditions of their own lives. They escape into following the fashions of consumption or showing avid interest in the pseudolife created by the mass media. And some take to more direct forms of narcosis such as alcoholism, promiscuity, or boredom. The top leaders and their lesser satellites struggle for control over the terms of people's lives. Meanwhile, the people perish.

CASE HISTORY OF A DECISION

What could be more obvious than the need for medical care? And what could be simpler than the task of replacing an outmoded, inadequate hospital building that is already overcrowded in all its wards and clinics? Especially does this seem necessary when it is a public hospital, the only hospital serving an area where a vast majority of low-income people live and will continue to live, where the population is concentrated at the two ends of the age scale, with a preponderance of births, childhood ailments, and geriatric cases. Yet the experience of one urban area that tried to secure a replacement for an eighty-year-old municipal hospital shows how complex are the forces that enter into the making of a single, seemingly obvious decision.

Elected officials had been promising the 200,000 residents of the area a new hospital for twenty years. Every election had seen the renewal of the promise, yet every year's budget failed to produce the desired results. Finally, in desperation the residents of the area, as individuals and in groups, began buttonholing officials, testifying at hearings, and rallying support for the promised hospital building. It was only as they sought to talk with those who had the final say on this particular decision that they began to realize how many forces were working to keep their hospital from becoming a reality.

The national organization of the medical profession

was opposed to the use of foreign interns as aides on hospital staffs, and their success in this campaign eliminated half the hospital's medical personnel; without replacements the commissioner of hospitals felt it impossible to staff the old, inadequate building, let alone a new one. The staff of the city's largest municipal hospital center wanted improvements for their facilities and opposed using the money for a replacement to a neighborhood hospital. In addition, the medical schools of the city refused to affiliate their students with the neighborhood hospital, preferring to have "interesting cases," the kind that are found in ward beds, not private rooms, brought to a central place for their students to observe and work with, rather than have the students scatter to hospitals nearer the patients' homes. So much for the medical pyramid.

An advisory group set up to make recommendations on the overall hospital picture in the city also recommended against the hospital's replacement, primarily because the group was heavily weighted with representatives of voluntary hospitals supported by private philanthropy, and the representatives of private health and hospitalization plans. Both wanted to see expansion of public aid to existing voluntary hospitals and a decrease in beds in municipal hospitals. The closing of an outmoded municipal hospital building seemed better to them than its replacement with a modern building. So much for the welfare pyramid.

The elected officials who had the final say on appropriating funds for hospitals and could give the red or green light to this particular project also proved to have their objections. Some just did not want to spend any money unless they had to. Others were afraid that the disfavor of voters who would have to be moved from the site on which a new building was to be built would prove more potent than the objections of those denied adequate facilities in their own neighborhood. Still others were unwilling to see one section of the city get a hospital replacement when other areas needed new buildings too. So much for the political pyramid.

Then, at every hearing on the budget there were the groups that wanted real estate taxes kept as low as possible, that wished to see business and commerce given every encouragement, that considered any additional expenditures in the area of health and welfare to be "a waste of the taxpayer's money." These groups, supported by the editorial pages and news columns of the city's press, continually plugged away at the theme that no new hospital was needed. The old one should be closed, they said, and existing facilities could more than take care of the ward and clinic patients. So much for the business pyramid.

Who was for tearing down the antiquated hospital building and replacing it with a modern structure? Only the 200,000 residents of the area, who would use the new hospital, and their organizations and representatives. Only the large numbers of young mothers, many of them newcomers to the city, whose babies would be born there. Only the school children who would receive treatment there. Only the adults who could not afford the price of the voluntary hospitals, even in a city-sponsored ward bed. Only the scores of older people who needed to receive treatment close to home. And all of these live at the base of the pyramids of power.

This is the case history of one decision among the thousands that are made every year in a metropolitan area. What seems from the outside to be a simple, obvious matter becomes on closer inspection a hornet's nest of conflicting interests and attitudes. The decision to build a replacement that would meet the health needs of 200,000 people proves to run directly counter to the desires and intentions of those most deeply concerned about the issue of hospitals, the medical profession and the welfare field. In addition, this decision raises serious repercussions in the structures of politics and business.

Even more important, each of the groups involved in the pattern of forces out of which a decision will be made sees the problem only in terms of its own definition of the component factors. The autonomy of each of the pyramids involved means that each is well insulated from considering the factors that are important to other groups. The medical profession considers only what is best for existing hospital personnel and convenience in medical education. The welfare field considers only its own financial stringencies and the institutions for which it is responsible. The politicians try to weigh voter against voter. Business and real estate interests are most influenced by tax rates. For every group that has some control over the final decision, the primary factor is not the health care of 200,000 people; it is rather the threat posed by the proposed hospital replacement to their own projects and position. This is the legacy of compartmentalization in our modern cities.

If this case history seems too forced in its portrayal of a large area of human need without an adequate champion and in its demonstration that the very structures and authorities which are supposed to be concerned about that need actually respond to the demands of other claims, let the reader choose any one of the thousands of significant decisions that are being made this year in his city. Let him search out the officials and groups who have a voice in making that decision. And let him see if the causes of their actions are as simple as they appear when viewed from the outside. And let him also discover the grounds on which their final choices are made. He will be surprised to learn that complexity and compartmentalization are the rule, not the exception, in the life of every city. Also, he will probably have to acknowledge that the pyramids of power which exist in other metropolitan areas are a feature of the social landscape in his own city as well.

HERE IS THE STEEPLE

Commentators on urban affairs often note the fact that skyscrapers and taller office and apartment buildings in the modern city almost completely obliterate the church steeple. Look at a picture of any nineteenth-century American city. If it was a seaport, behind the forest of masts at the waterfront can be seen a forest of steeples and towers marking the meetinghouses of the various congregations; if it was an inland city, only those buildings which were built on higher ground seem to stand taller than the steeples. Yet, even when seen from the air, the twentieth-century city gives almost no hint of the location of its places of worship. And seen from the ground by those on its sidewalks and streets, the city also obscures the buildings which are the base of operations for members of the church fellowship. The average passerby scarcely notices the church's building, and he is seldom urged by its presence alone to enter and worship or take part in the life of its people.

The church is not the building, we say; it is the people of God who worship in that building and who witness to the work of God in every part of life. In such a case, it does not matter if the building is lost among the others in the city, so long as the church's members do not disappear when the city is looked at as a social organism. Seen from the outside, the church as an institution is certainly a part of the city's life. The daily papers always print a church page on Saturday with announcements and advertisements from the churches; and the Monday morning edition will often report what was said in a few sermons the day before. From time to time, statements by various church spokesmen appear in the news columns, while the news reports of a religious holiday would not be complete without pictures and stories reporting attendance at worship. Yet the press shows only the surface and gives a superficial impression that the churches are a vital part of the city's life.

When one goes inside the social structure of the city looking for some evidence of the impact of the church upon the wider society, the picture is not so heartening. Although many of those who stand in the top echelons of leadership and make the key decisions are churchmen— that is, worship with and belong to a local church fellowship—almost none of them takes active leadership in the church's life, leaving her affairs to subordinates, those who operate at lower levels with matters considered to be of less importance. Thus, in its own institutional life the church must operate as a subordinate institution, a lesser partner dependent for much of her own existence on the leaders of state and business. To be sure, these leaders feel the church is "a good thing"; there is no persecution in American society. Quite the opposite; American religious institutions are established and recognized by the wider society of which they are a part.

Yet the churches are expected to live and work at a point removed from the center of focus of the city's life. This can be seen in the willingness of those in positions of prestige, authority, and power to leave direction of the church's affairs to underlings. It can be seen even more clearly when the churches seek to have an influence on the decision-making process. Almost no ministers and few active churchmen are included in the basic decisions. And church leaders, whether they be prominent laymen or the professional clergy, have relatively little influence with political and business leaders who organize and direct the city. It is not just the steeples that are obscured in the modern city; the whole institution of the church as part of the city is peripheral to the mainstream of its life.

OPEN THE DOOR, SEE ALL THE PEOPLE

Even in the face of this insignificance as an institution, we could argue that the church, as a fellowship of God's people, does not have to be known in the seats of power, so long as its members can be seen living out their lives with others who are caught in the tangled web of the city. The church does not need to be highly placed among the pyramids of power, so long as its activity can be discerned at the base of those pyramids. The church does not need to be providing basic organization for society, so long as its members take their full role in the shifting complex of forces that make up the final pattern of people's life in the city.

But once again, even when we view the life of the city from underneath, we are not able to see the church clearly. From time to time we can see the clergy among those who play out the wider struggle for control on the local scene. When the local church is directly challenged or its people feel a decision involves them deeply, the church itself may enter the fray. But this is most likely to be in connection with issues like the location of a liquor license or the use of gambling methods for money-raising by other religious groups. Even the individual members of local congregations become almost invisible in this day-to-day struggle for the form and content of urban life. Few churchmen dare to enter the public arena in the name of their faith, and many of those who become too deeply involved in problems of politics, business, labor, social welfare, and the like are criticized and cut off by their own congregations for becoming too involved in matters "outside the church."

The final picture of the city, then, is all too clear. The buildings that spread from the city's heart to the farthest suburb do not represent the city at all; they are only the shell in which this complicated social organism lives. The press and other media of communication do not give us a clear picture of the sources of stability and change in this vast, interconnected complex. For these we must look at the decisions which set the basic policy, decisions which are made by a limited group of people, primarily concentrated in the fields of business and government. Yet, as we come closer to decisions in most areas, we discover that they are made out of the interplay and conflict among many contending forces, each having its stake in the final solution and each thinking primarily in its own terms. As for the churches and their members, they seem far away from this basic power structure at almost every point. Living their lives within its sway, they are seldom to be found in the place where decisions are made or conflict is going on or forces are contending to have their limited understanding become the basis of public policy. In a word, the church is virtually invisible when we look at the city's power structure.

Does this mean that God is not here either? Are his work and will as obscured and obliterated as the steeples of the meetinghouses? If he is considered to be confined within the walls of a church building, then God is as absent in the modern city as his church. But if he moves out into the whole life of the world, then he becomes as much a part of the life of those outside the church's fellowship as of those inside it. And even the top leaders who dwell in the pyramids of business and government are not exempt from his influence, and the countless multitudes who live in humble obscurity as part of the faceless crowds are beneficiaries of his protection. This is the final truth about the city—whether seen from the air or the ground, from the outside or the inside or underneath: the church may be obscure and relatively powerless, but the God in whom we Christians believe is Lord over even the mightiest city and its metropolitan regions.

Chapter II

The Powers That Be: God and the Status Quo

THE CITY IN GOD'S CREATION

WE OFTEN HEAR THE CITY AND ITS LIFE DESCRIBED as if it were man's creation set over against God's creation in nature. According to this view, God created the stars, the earth, the sea, and all the living things that grow, move, creep, crawl, swim, and fly therein; but the life of human society, being a part of culture, is man's creation in complete independence from God. Others may speak of the city as if the towers of the skyscrapers, the asphalt of the streets, and the other fruits of man's handiwork cut us off from God, but this is a blasphemous and unbiblical way to view the situation.

In truth, the life of the city and its people is as much a part of God's creation as the planets or the lilies or the bugs. Both stories of Creation in Genesis affirm that man was created to live in society, and that the most important fact about his life is not his relation to nature and the universe but his relation to his fellows and to God. "Male and female he created *them*. And God blessed them, and God said to them, 'Be fruitful and multiply, and fill the earth and subdue it.'" (Gen. 1:27–28, italics mine.) "The Lord God said, 'It is not good that the man should be alone; I will make him a helper fit for him.'" (Gen.

20

2:18.) In the prehistoric memories preserved in the record of the descendants of Cain (Gen. 4:17–26) and the confusion of language after Babel (Gen. 11:1–9), the life of man in society and all his technology are seen as part of creation, though often in rebellion against God's will.

The God who made the heavens and the earth also made the man who makes the city. We do not find it difficult to understand that the good Lord has provided us with water when we come upon a clear, bubbling, mountain spring while hiking in the wilderness. However, it is harder to comprehend that he, with the aid of man's ingenuity and strength, has also provided us with the water that flows so freely from a faucet in the middle of the city. Whether the source of this water is in deep rock fountains under the city or in springs at the bottom of a nearby lake or river, or in far-off streams or reservoirs, it has all been furnished as part of God's creation. And he has also given intelligence and understanding to the engineers who design the aqueducts, pumping stations, and purification plants, as well as strength and endurance to the laborers who hew out the great tunnels and lay the pipes. Man's works of creation should never be allowed to obscure the fact that they are founded upon God's great work of Creation.

But the city, like other parts of human culture, always stands in danger of forgetting its Maker and its Lord. This may explain why the Hebrew nomads with their tents and flocks were so prone to describe man's sin and pride in terms of the life of cities—Babel, which men built to make a name for themselves (Gen. 11:4); Sodom and Gomorrah, the cities of the plain that were destroyed because of their evil reputation (Gen. 19:13); great Babylon, whose greatest king, Nebuchadnezzar, gloried in the mighty power by which he had built its walls until he learned the lesson that " 'the Most High rules the kingdom of men and gives it to whom he will'" (Dan. 4:29–33). The greater the city, the greater the temptation to forget that the Most High rules the city.

Yet the faith we profess has never seen cities solely in terms of their sin, for that is a part of human life in the loneliest wasteland as much as in the densest metropolis. The Bible also speaks of fulfillment and redemption in terms of the life of cities. Jerusalem, the city of David, was built so that the people of Israel might have their own place and be disturbed no more. Here were found both the seat of government and the house of the Lord. (II Sam., chs. 5 to 7; I Kings, chs. 6 to 8.) Of this city the psalmist could sing:

> For the Lord has chosen Zion;
>   he has desired it for his habitation:
> "This is my resting place for ever;
>   here I will dwell, for I have desired it."
>   (Ps. 132: 13–14.)

The prophet Ezekiel could see the Lord's final deliverance in terms of a restored world, with Jerusalem and the Temple at its very center (Ezek., chs. 40 to 48). And the closing picture of salvation in the New Testament is "the holy city, new Jerusalem, coming down out of heaven from God, prepared as a bride adorned for her husband" (Rev. 21:2). Cities, like the men who inhabit them, display both the wretchedness and the glory of God's Creation.

THE POWERS THAT BE

God is the city's Maker and its Lord. But we see other makers and other lords closer at hand. The water may flow from its hidden springs at the command of the Creator, but we see only the water faucet and the meter reader. The social order within which we live our lives may have been instituted by the Lord, but we know most directly the rule of the various authorities who occupy the pyramids of power. This situation has been common to urban man in all ages and caused the apostle Paul to write thus to Christians who inhabited imperial Rome, the greatest city of ancient times:

Let every person be subject to the governing authorities. For there is no authority except from God, and those that exist [KJV: "the powers that be"] have been instituted by God. Therefore he who resists the authorities resists what God has appointed, and those who resist will incur judgment. For rulers are not a terror to good conduct, but to bad. Would you have no fear of him who is in authority? Then do what is good, and you will receive his approval, for he is God's servant for your good. (Rom. 13:1-4.)

Power (Gr. *exousia;* Lat. *auctoritas,* from which comes the English word "authority") is first a possession of God. He is the one whom we can describe as all-powerful, almighty. Whether we speak of his far-flung power over the reaches of the universe or his more intimate sway over the hearts of men, we are still describing his infinite Lordship. God's power and authority are the only rule that bows to no other ruler. In a very real sense, when we are talking about the "power structure" of the world, we must start at this point: fundamental power is in the hands of God. Paul has put it rightly: "There is no authority [power] except from God."

But we see a power structure that lies nearer to us, the host of lesser powers that govern our lives. These are "the powers that be," the governing authorities who determine the direction of our life in the city. Their decisions are the ones that are crucial in the metropolitan area, and they—not God—are the ones to whom the apostle bids us be subject. We are to obey their decrees, says Paul; we are to abide by their decisions; we are to accept the framework they create for the body politic. We are to be subject to the powers that be, not for their own sake, but because "those that exist have been instituted by God."

How strange it is to hear politicians and businessmen, union officials and school superintendents, and all the other leaders, large and small, on the pyramids of power called "God's servant for your good"! We are far more accustomed to the title "public servant," by which we mean anyone who serves the people at large. But the idea that a man cannot be a public servant if God has not first allowed him to be his servant is strange to the ears of modern Americans. We think that the ruler has seized, or even created, this power for himself; or else we think that he has been allowed to have it as a trust by the people over whom he exercises authority. But we forget that the consent of the governed is necessary, not because all power rests with the governed, but because all power rests with God, who stands above both rulers and ruled, governors and governed, the powers that be and the relatively powerless multitude whose future hangs on their decisions.

Paul could call the authorities of Rome "servants of God," even "ministers of God," because they established and administered public order in that great metropolis on behalf of God, who exercises the final dominion. We may find it hard to comprehend that the Roman emperor, tribunes, Senate, judges, officers, soldiers, and a host of lesser officials—all of them pagans—could have been servants and ministers of God. These titles are now reserved for the faithful and those who bear office within the fellowship of faith, the church. But Paul is trying to make it clear that God created human society and that he expects men to live within the framework of a social order. Those who create and maintain this order are doing God's work; they are his servants, his ministers.

POWER—OFFICIAL AND UNOFFICIAL

In imperial Rome there was only one seat of power, the government of the Roman emperor. For this reason, commentators down through the ages have tended to identify the powers that be with the state, the official government for the governed. However, our look at the modern city has shown that we now have a broader government, official and unofficial. Many in the pyramids of power occupy their positions, not through election or some other formal process, but because they have acquired the knowledge or seniority or influence necessary to exercise authority. Although the political pyramid is an important part of this power structure, the powers that be are not all political.

All the classical commentators on the life of society gave their primary attention to the state. Plato's philosopher-kings in *The Republic* were to wield political power, as were the rulers in Aristotle's *Politics*. The medieval philosophers from Augustine to Aquinas, and the Renaissance and Enlightenment thinkers from Dante and Machiavelli to Rousseau and Voltaire, all had the state in mind when they were thinking about public order. Likewise, Martin Luther and John Calvin, in framing their respective views of civil conduct, were thinking of the magistrates and the state when they interpreted Rom., ch. 13. The same was true of the Independents and other Puritan theologians, who laid the groundwork for much of our American understanding of government. And the debates of our country's Founding Fathers, whether in *The Federalist* papers or their other writings, all assumed that, once the foundation of the social order had been laid in the republican form of government, all other problems of society would assume their proper place under law.

Yet we now face a situation in the life of our urban centers where the unofficial power exercised by those who are not part of the state is fully as vital to the maintenance of public order as the official power exercised by the state. Our government is both broader and narrower than the classical description of the powers that be. It is broader, because we find, added to the elected and appointed officials, a whole host of unofficial authorities, each of whom shares in the shaping of society. It is at the same time narrower, because a very limited group, located primarily in finance and government, can make the basic decisions which set the limits within which the rest of society functions; and many of these decisions fall quite outside the structures of the state.

Therefore, we must include the leaders of all the pyramids of power in the life of the city as a part of the powers that be. In their complexity and compartmentalization, they all bear a share of the task of ordering the life of the city's inhabitants. And we must remember that the state and its machinery does not contain all the servants of God, all the ministers who exercise his authority over the lives of men. Still further, we must be sure that we do not limit the powers that have influence over the life of the metropolis to those which have responsibility within the city limits. The many authorities of the whole metropolitan region (fourteen hundred separate governmental structures in metropolitan New York alone!)— not to mention state governments, which keep to themselves many basic decisions for even the largest cities, and the Federal Government, which carries an increasing share of responsibility—all have their role to play. The picture is a complicated one, indeed: official and unofficial powers sharing authority; governments at many levels all having their say about the city's affairs. For the modern city, this is what we mean when we speak of being subject to the powers that be.

THE PURPOSE OF THE STATUS QUO

The powers that be, then, are those who actually govern, those who possess and exercise authority over the lives of the city's inhabitants. Another way to describe them would be to call them the *status quo,* a Latin phrase meaning the state of things as they are. The status quo, the established order, is necessary for human life in society. Without a sense of order and a framework within which to work, no part of the far-flung life of the metropolis would have any coherence or purpose, except that which it makes for itself. Without a status quo, the whole breaks down into its component parts and loses its place as an institution of God.

Christian thought, basing itself on Paul's argument in Rom., ch. 13, has customarily had a more limited understanding of the status quo. "Would you have no fear of him who is in authority?" asks Paul.

Then do what is good and you will receive his approval, for he is God's servant for your good. But if you do wrong, be afraid, for he does not bear the sword in vain; he is the servant of God to execute his wrath on the wrongdoer. Therefore one must be subject, not only to avoid God's wrath but also for the sake of conscience. (Rom. 13:3–5.)

The governing authorities, according to the classical Christian position, have the primary purpose of restraining sin. Bearing the power to rule and punish ("the sword"), these magistrates are to keep men from wrongdoing, and thus to help them fulfill their obligations under the law of the Ten Commandments. Martin Luther, operating on this assumption, saw the life of society divided into the complementary, yet separate compartments of law and gospel. The law, man's civic duties in God's creation under the Ten Commandments, was to be enforced by the power of the state (the governing authorities), while the gospel, man's free response to God's redeeming grace, was to be preached and experienced within the fellowship of the church. The social order had its proper place, but only for the expression of God's wrath against man's sin.

This view of God's provision for mankind assigns only a negative role to the status quo: the restraint and punishment of sin. However, we must add a positive role that is not included in Paul's advice to the Christians at Rome. The inhabitant of the city needs the status quo not only to keep him from wrongdoing but also to provide him with the opportunity for right living.

Understood this way, the status quo not only restrains the citizens of an urban area from sin and wrongdoing; it also provides the framework within which their own decisions and actions can achieve some measure of God's purpose for human life in society. Though God is the Creator of all life, man himself is the one who fashions his social life. He does this by using the materials furnished by God in the created order and his own God-given intelligence. But there cannot be free expression of human creativity unless the society within which we live has coherence and its own order. Once the framework has been set and the basic decisions made, then each man has the possibility of bringing his own contribution to the common life.

Without a commonly understood way to live his life in relation to his fellows and to God, the inhabitant of a city is faced with the impossible task of creating meaning for everything which he does. His own share of the common life becomes like a piece of living tissue ripped from the body that gave it nourishment and reason for being, placed in a test tube and leading a maimed, useless existence until it is joined once again to another host body. We can truly say that if the banker does not help maintain a sound economy in the city, then the taxi driver cannot fully do his job of transportation; if the commissioner of police does not ensure that his officers safeguard the property and rights of the citizens, then the schoolteacher is limited in her work of education; if the planning commission does not have a coherent idea of the way in which the city is to develop, then the humblest newcomer is open to the basest exploitation and prevented from sending down his roots. The status quo is given to us by God not only for the restraint of evil but also for the ordering and release of human possibility and creativity.

THE ANARCHY OF URBAN LIFE

During the heyday of Nazi and Fascist totalitarianism and conquest, Archibald MacLeish composed a radio drama, *The Fall of a City*. Through the use of radio news flashes, he described the progress of a conqueror in shining armor from the distant horizon up to the walls of the city and into the central square, where the inhabitants are waiting in fear and panic. The climax is reached when the conquering leader opens the visor of his helmet, revealing that the suit of armor is empty; the city has been conquered by its own imagination and is left with no one to lead it. Thus, MacLeish tried to state in symbolic terms the essential anarchy of totalitarianism.

Although it has never been invested with the demonic ideological overtones of totalitarianism, there is a comparable anarchy in the life of most of our largest American metropolitan areas. In election after election we see the contending conquerors for the office of mayor proceed toward the city with their way prepared by an avalanche of press releases, radio and television spot announcements, speeches and personal appearances. They promise that "if I am elected," all the complex problems of the vast metropolitan region with its hundreds of thousands of people will be solved by the energy and determination of their administration. Then, once elected, they lift the visor of their helmet and show that their claim to leadership has been an empty boast. Elected leaders can work on those problems which clamor for priority or which fall most naturally to hand, but they seldom intend to take firm hold of the whole government of a city. Therefore, mayors often occupy the office, giving the impression that the city has a central administration, while actually leaving whole areas of the city's life to flourish—or wither—on their own.

A feature of the central square of the city in MacLeish's radio drama was the hulking pyramid of the temple in which the priests were performing their symbolic exercises. At the height of the action, when the conqueror enters the central square, the priests disappear within their sacred enclave, leaving the multitudes outside to their fate. Here again we can see a parable of urban life where each of the pyramids of power retreats within its own structure, leaving no one to be concerned for the overall view and the more general task of giving order and coherence to the whole. As in the case history described in the previous chapter, each group of contending forces becomes so concerned for its own survival and the achievement of its own goals that the primary purpose can be completely lost to sight.

Anarchy in the life of a modern American city is still further encouraged by the host of authorities who must contend with one another to establish the basic outlines of community in the metropolitan region. In the metropolitan area itself, city government goes only as far as the city limits, yet city problems do not. Therefore, many of the most stubborn situations complicating the life of urban residents—for example, the question of adequate transportation to and from the city on roads and rapid-transit facilities—cannot begin to be solved because there are so many different authorities in surrounding villages, towns, counties, and even satellite cities who must have a share in the solution. The problems of a city are often the problems of its whole metropolitan region, yet there is almost no city in the United States that has any regional organization to work on them.

Another complicating factor is the rural dominance of state government in every state of the union. In cities all over the country you hear constant reference to "downstate" or "upstate," because many of the primary conditions of urban life are set by the vote of legislators representing small towns and the less populated parts of the state. Recent Federal court decisions have called dramatic attention to the way in which a rural legislator, representing a few thousand people, possesses a voting strength equal to that of a city representative elected by ten times as many voters. Time and again we have seen the school systems of great cities in various parts of the United States, sometimes enrolling more pupils than all the rest of the state's educational system, completely at the mercy of a state administration that is far more concerned about consolidated rural schools and bus service than about overcrowding and problems of integration in city schools. Basic indifference to the city's problems on the part of a state government dominated by the rural areas can also foster urban anarchy.

Finally, the increasing role of Federal Government in urban affairs also tends to place the power to decide outside the hands of those who are most intimately acquainted with the problems of a particular metropolitan area. Federal agencies operating under the authority of Federal legislation, especially in the fields of housing and redevelopment, have grown in the scope of their operation in cities. Often the number of Federal employees working in offices in a city will exceed the number of employees in municipal or state service in the same city. Increased Federal appropriations for city problems have contributed their share to urban anarchy by making it necessary to refer many problems for final solution to Washington, D.C.

THE NEED TO CREATE COMMUNITY

When Paul urged the Roman Christians to be subject to the powers that be, he assumed that a human community was already in existence there. God intended for men to live in society, and the governing authorities are his vicegerents in the ordering and maintenance of that society. We have already shown that Paul was not speaking to a situation in which there was an unofficial government operating in concert with the state. We must also emphasize that he was not speaking to a situation in which there was virtual anarchy (Gr. *anarchia,* without a head, having no ruler). The modern city with its lack of community and multiplicity of rulers presents a different picture from the one to which Paul was speaking.

Where the early church was called by the apostle to recognize its duty to obey established authority, the church in the modern city is often called upon to assist in creating community so that some measure of authority can be established over urban life. The typical slum block, with its overflowing garbage cans, its overpowering list of building and fire violations, its pockets of illicit and criminal activity, is a perfect illustration of urban anarchy and the need to create community. The residents of the block may have developed a "live and let live" attitude that makes their life bearable, but the underlying emotions are suspicion and fear, symbolized by locks and bars on apartment doors and windows; apathy and inertia, demonstrated in the unwillingness of residents to be concerned for sanitation or repairs outside their own quarters; rootlessness and anomie, that limbo state of personality into which men fall when there is lack of opportunity and hope. From the outside a crowded slum may appear to be teeming with vital, exotic life; but from the inside it is a community that exists in a state of suspended animation, never fully reaching the possibilities of social living.

A closer examination of the conditions creating that slum block will reveal that it lies in one of the sections of the city which have been placed on a blacklist by the bankers and others concerned with the financing of real estate. Mortgages are not available at going market rates for improvement and renovation, forcing owners to go to unofficial money sources for loans at exorbitant rates. Very few of the landlords live in the area or in their own buildings, leaving the management to agents who collect rents and try to provide the least service possible. These are the sections of the city most likely to be inhabited by newcomers to the city—minority groups whose incomes are constantly at the mercy of the business cycle because they are the last to be hired and the first to be fired. Yet they are also the sections of the city where the machinery of the political parties is most likely to be in the hands of older residents who continue to cling to their petty privileges while ignoring the situation of the newcomers, whose presence they resent.

There are the ingredients of a human community here —people, residences, the various services and groups that make up any society. But no one has pointed out that the raw materials must have a recipe and be mixed together in proper proportions and finally be baked at an endurable temperature for a period of time before that community comes into existence. In many situations in the modern city, the Christian is first called on to assist in the process of creating community. Working at the neighborhood level to bring people together around their common problems, and working at higher levels to interest the established authorities in those matters which are their proper responsibility, he should be trying to ensure that this block or neighborhood or district begins to function as a full society, rather than as the maimed and stunted body it has become. Many times the need to create community precedes the need to assure respect for proper authorities or to add further unsettling change in a city neighborhood. Until there are rulers and established authority, community cannot be said to exist here. And social life is difficult without the society of which it is a part.

PLANNING AND THE CREATION OF COMMUNITY

The importance of the status quo, and its place in the creation and maintenance of human society as a part of God's creation, can be seen in the problems raised by the efforts of city planners to lay out the pattern of the city's future. No one denies that the physical structure of most of our American cities stands in dire need of being replaced and renewed. In addition, the rapid increase of city populations and their dispersion to outlying residential areas in suburbia and exurbia have created a need for additional services and a necessity to plan for the whole metropolitan region rather than the city proper. Few would envy the city planners their task as they try to develop a rational, livable plan for the city that will meet the needs of the population twenty-five, fifty, and even a hundred years hence.

Suburban residents argue that their communities should be preserved, and are able to divert proposed changes so that their residential enclaves are not affected. They succeed in maintaining the community they know without contributing anything to the community that shall be. Modest homeowners near the center of a city also seek to preserve their present state, but in the name of progress they may see all they have created swept away in a project of "urban improvement." They have been totally sacrificed for the shape of the city of the future, yet little has been done to guarantee their place in that future community. As for the slum residents, they have neither present community nor the assurance of a future in urban society. In the name of "slum clearance" thousands of their numbers have been uprooted and made into native displaced persons in our metropolitan areas since the close of World War II. Because they do not have a voice in the decisions, the low-income citizens are urged to accept whatever place they are offered for residence, no matter how substandard or inconvenient.

The city planner is not God. He cannot know whether he chooses wisely when he allows pressure and prestige to override his vision of an interrelated metropolitan area. Neither can he be sure that the new boundaries he draws for the people's dwelling place will be more satisfactory than the old. Nor can he plead the cause of the needy and their place in society if the city as a whole seems determined to deny they even exist. The city planner's vision is limited—even as is the vision of the political leaders, the financial leaders, and all the other powers that be, official and unofficial, who govern the lives of the city's people. Yet the planner and the other governing authorities cannot escape that task which God has placed in their hands: the creation and maintenance of community, even among so large a population as that of a metropolitan area. The city's Maker and Lord is God. He will bind up the people's wounds and amend the leaders' mistakes, but he will not relieve any governing authority or any member of the populace of his share in this work of creation that is the life of the city.

Chapter III

Prophesying at Bethel:
God and Social Criticism

The City Under God's Judgment

THE CITIES OF MEN, LIKE THE REST OF GOD'S CREA-
tion, live always in the face of the Lord's judgment upon
their sin. No human being and no human society fully
realizes the purposes for which God has made them. If
this is true in the mountains and farms and woodlands,
we cannot expect that it will be any different in the city's
crowded streets. The picture of wicked Babylon, the har-
lot city with her sins heaped high as heaven, may have
been too large a part of rural thinking in our American
past and contributed to the myth that sin has a peculiar
affinity for cities. Yet this picture helps us to remember
that, in spite of their technological and cultural advan-
tages, the cities of our land—if only because they represent a greater concentration of population—certainly contain their proportionate share of human sin.

The city has been given to man for the nurture of
human society: for the development of community, for
the fostering of enterprise and culture, for the release of
man's creativity, and above all, for the true worship of
God. The same word used throughout the New Testament for the church's rituals of sacred worship within the

fellowship (Gr. *leitourgia,* liturgy, service, ministry) is also used more commonly to refer to public service rendered in the everyday life of the community at large. The city is literally intended for the service of God, in the widest sense of that word. This service is rendered as fully by the minister who collects taxes and dispenses welfare as by the minister who preaches from the pulpit and distributes the elements at the Lord's Supper. The city's inhabitants worship as truly when they give their full measure of work on the job and accord respect to their neighbor as when they sing hymns with a full voice in their meetinghouse and show love to the brethren within the Christian fellowship. God has brought cities into being so that they may realize true society. Their leaders and inhabitants are not only to recognize the need for community; they are also commissioned by God to bring it into being. This is their worship.

Yet the truth of the matter is that cities do not offer full worship to God. The service of their inhabitants is always partial, because their pride and personal desires get in the way of fulfillment of the Lord's will for their own lives and the life of the city. A visit to a city police station in the middle of the night or to the magistrates' court in the cold light of the next day should be enough to convince even the most kindly intentioned observer that the Lord does not receive his true worship here. Two men, bleeding with knife slashes, are brought in after a tavern brawl. A frantic mother comes in to the sergeant's desk to report that her thirteen-year-old daughter has stayed out all night and not come home. Policemen escort a shivering burglar who has been found entering a house by the rear fire escape. A belligerent husband and his battered wife are brought in after a marital scuffle that has wakened the neighbors and frightened their children. The parade of human misery and wrongdoing across the pages of the police blotter is never-ending—pimps and prostitutes, drug addicts and pushers, thieves and extortionists, the violent, the crafty, and the perverted. These are the ledgers in which the named sins are written, but the unwritten record, known only to God and those whose lives have been affected, is far longer and more terrible. The sin of the city's inhabitants cannot be hidden or ignored.

At once more obvious and less recognized is the partial service rendered by those who have been called to be God's ministers for the good of the city's people, the leaders who bear special responsibilities. Everyone is shocked when a municipal official turns his position of public trust to private gain, when members of the police force who are to restrain the criminal turn to crime themselves, when the banker who extends credit to others proves to have no credit himself. Such breaches of the leaders' responsibilities to the whole community are obvious and easy to detect. However, there are subtler sins, less easy to recognize, that exact an even more painful toll from the common life. A trained eye can read them in the figures of a municipal budget or the balance sheet of a charitable agency, in the statistics of a census tract or a health area, in the look of the roofs and basements of houses, or the look of shoes at the employment office. The impact of these failures of leadership is measured most tragically and personally in the cries of a mother whose child has died for lack of proper treatment in a city hospital, in the weary voice of a wage earner explaining his situation to the welfare worker, in the half-incoherent account of an adolescent trying to make himself plain to the probation officer. The record of the sins of the city's leaders is here too—known fully to God alone, yet not completely obscured from human eyes.

PROPHESYING AT BETHEL

When the prophet Amos was taken from his flocks and sycamore trees, the Lord said to him, " 'Go, prophesy to my people Israel' " (Amos 7:14–15). Amos went directly to Bethel, the central place of worship in Israel and the sanctuary of its ruler, King Jeroboam. Here he delivered the word of the Lord that showed the people of Israel their sins:

He showed me: behold, the Lord was standing beside a wall built with a plumb line, with a plumb line in his hand. And the Lord said to me, "Amos, what do you see?" And I said, "A plumb line." Then the Lord said,
"Behold, I am setting a plumb line
　in the midst of my people Israel;
　I will never again pass by them;
the high places of Isaac shall be made desolate,
　and the sanctuaries of Israel shall be laid waste,
　and I will rise against the house of Jeroboam with the
　　sword."

(Amos 7:7–9.)

Like a wall that is measured against a straight plumb line to see if it has been laid level and true, the life of Israel was being measured by the standard of God's justice.

The reaction of Bethel's inhabitants to Amos' words is not described in the Bible, but we do know the reaction of the city's leaders. Amaziah, the priest of Bethel, sent word to King Jeroboam at his capital city of Samaria, saying, " 'Amos has conspired against you in the midst of the house of Israel; the land is not able to bear all his words' " (Amos 7:10). The governing authorities do not like to be challenged where everybody can see and hear, "in the midst of the house of Israel." And it is easy for those who are in power to interpret every challenge to the rightness of their decisions and policies as a conspiracy. Therefore, the priest told the king that Amos was "conspiring" against him, when the prophet was actually delivering that very word which the king most needed to hear.

Amaziah, the priest of Bethel, also went to the prophet Amos, and tried to get him to leave town and do his prophesying elsewhere:

O seer, go, flee away to the land of Judah, and eat bread there, and prophesy there; but never again prophesy at Bethel, for it is the king's sanctuary, and it is a temple of the kingdom. (Amos 7:12-13.)

Amaziah wanted Amos to go back to the Southern Kingdom of Judah and to leave Bethel alone, for it was the center of the powers that be, king and priests. But Amos knew that this was exactly where the Lord's word of judgment and criticism had to be delivered—not in the hills of Judah, but in the city of Bethel; not to his fellow herdsmen and dressers of sycamore trees, but to King Jeroboam, Amaziah the priest, and the citizens of Bethel. Even though his message was not wanted and went unheeded, it was important that Amos should prophesy at Bethel. God's justice was intended for this city and its inhabitants.

In his prophecy Amos was very specific about the sins of Israel:

They sell the righteous for silver,
    and the needy for a pair of shoes—
they . . . trample the head of the poor into the dust of the
        earth,
    and turn aside the way of the afflicted; . . .
they lay themselves down beside every altar
    upon garments taken in pledge;
and in the house of their God they drink
    the wine of those who have been fined.

(Amos 2:6-8.)

He spoke about the wives of the rich merchants and other men of privilege who were living in luxury on the profits extorted from the poor and needy:

Hear this word, you cows of Bashan,
  who are in the mountain of Samaria,
who oppress the poor, who crush the needy,
  who say to their husbands, "Bring, that we may drink!"
The Lord God has sworn by his holiness
  that, behold, the days are coming upon you,
when they shall take you away with hooks,
  even the last of you with fishhooks.

(Amos 4:1–2.)

Although these women were able to have anything they desired, the time was coming when they would be led away captive with hooks, as was the custom of conquerors in the ancient Middle East.

The prophet Amos had come to Bethel to show the people of Israel their sins. He was particularly concerned, however, to speak to those who were in the positions of power, for they were well satisfied with their leadership and the material rewards it brought to them and their families. They were neglecting the needs of the rest of the people. In a time of prosperity and peace, they were overlooking the fact that much of their own well-being was secured at the expense of the poor, who could not obtain their just share and had even that which they owned taken away by exactions and bribes and legal proceedings (cf. Amos 5:10–12). The prophet was a critic who had to speak up on behalf of the Lord. And his word of criticism had to be brought to the seats of power, the sanctuary at Bethel and the king's house at Samaria.

GOD DESIRES JUSTICE

The heart of the message of Amos is his statement that the service God desires is justice in the life of the city, not the service of formal religion. Through the prophet, the Lord says:

I hate, I despise your feasts,
  and I take no delight in your solemn assemblies.

Even though you offer me your burnt offerings and cereal
    offerings,
  I will not accept them,
and the peace offerings of your fatted beasts
  I will not look upon.
Take away from me the noise of your songs;
  to the melody of your harps I will not listen.
But let justice roll down like waters,
  and righteousness like an ever-flowing stream.

(Amos 5:21–24.)

It is justice that God wants to see in the city. It is righteousness that he expects of its citizens.

We are accustomed to thinking of "justice" in terms of
the law courts and the philosophy textbooks. Justice, we
say, is when a man receives his just punishment or re-
ward under the law. Or again, justice is rendering to
every man his due. Although such definitions may have
in them some of the quality of justice about which Amos
was speaking, they are not truly God's justice.

God himself is just. This is the basis of justice.

I will proclaim the name of the Lord.
    Ascribe greatness to our God!
The Rock, his work is perfect;
    for all his ways are justice.
A God of faithfulness and without iniquity,
    just and right is he.

(Deut. 32:3–4.)

The justice that Amos is calling to roll down upon Israel
like waters, the righteousness that is to come upon Bethel
and Samaria like an ever-flowing stream, is the perfect
justice of God, who in all his ways is just and right. Divine justice, the plumb line of Amos' vision, is the measure by which the leaders of the city and all its inhabitants
are to be measured. Their human justice is truly just only
if it participates in his divine justice and righteousness.

This means that justice is not the result of compromise,

of the haggling back and forth between human antagonists who finally reach an adequate balance. In the metropolitan region justice is not that tolerable compromise which is worked out between contending groups when they agree to "live and let live." Rather, all the estates of the modern city are measured by the justice of God. He alone is perfect and just. "A God of faithfulness and without iniquity, just and right is he." The life of the city is expected to display the qualities of God's justice. Thus, whether the default occurs in the fabric of society or the affairs of one of its members, whether it springs from the rich and powerful or the poor and lowly, the Lord desires that it should be brought to judgment. The judgment of God is the bringing to light of all those ways in which the performance of society and its members fall short of the righteousness and justice of God.

CHALLENGE AND CRITICISM

Our modern cities do not have an Amos who can step into the main intersection of the downtown business district and hold the plumb line of divine judgment against all the millions of inhabitants who live and work in the homes, shops, factories, and offices that stretch for miles from that central spot. Even if they had such a prophet, the interaction of millions of people and their multiplicity of institutions and associations is so complex and the issues so specialized that the prophet's catalog of sins would be almost endless—even if he possessed the many kinds of technical knowledge necessary to find them out. Therefore, although there are times when the preacher in his pulpit or the newspaper editor at his typewriter aspires to the role of an Amos, we must recognize that the judgment of God is brought upon today's cities through more prosaic means. Although justice cannot be described as that result of the give-and-take of contending groups in which each man receives his due, we must acknowledge that this pattern of challenge and criticism is the process by which God's justice is known in the city's common life.

An irate group of parents appear at a board of education meeting to protest double sessions in their neighborhood school when classrooms stand half used in an adjacent area: they are the prophet bringing judgment to the school authorities. A picket line of maintenance employees march outside a charitable hospital to demand that their wages be raised above the subsistence level permitted nonprofit agencies: they are the prophet bringing judgment to the hospital's board and administration. A youth worker sits in a luncheonette with the officers of a fighting youth gang and lets them know that not only the police but their own parents and the other adults who live in the neighborhood will be doing all they can to prevent further violence and bloodshed: he is the prophet bringing judgment to this group of teen-agers dedicated to the worship of force. A long-winded, sharp-tongued individual shows up at the regular meeting of a community association and harangues the group about its "persecution" of landlords by continually championing the cause of tenants through housing clinics: he is the prophet bringing judgment upon those self-appointed prophets who sometimes assume that the welfare of the whole community is whatever they presume it to be.

"WHOM DO YOU REPRESENT?"

Whenever a delegation goes to visit a public official or to testify before a public hearing, when a group of tenants goes to see the landlord or a group of citizens goes to visit a prominent businessman or leader in one of the other pyramids of city life, they are likely to be asked the question, "Whom do you represent?" The implication is that they will be heard if they represent enough other people or groups possessing sufficient prestige and power.

Observers of the social scene agree that different groups of people concern themselves about decisions in the various spheres of life that make up a metropolitan area. When the issue under consideration is education, parents' groups and teachers' organizations can be counted on to raise their voices. When the problem concerns the welfare of children, another constellation of associations, professionals, and interested citizens comes forward to present its opinions. No public official—and no wielder of unofficial power—can expect to remain unchallenged. The power of pressure groups and of other sections of the powers that be exert a constant force shaping and molding his decisions. And, knowing whom they represent and their powers of reprisal, the city leader is going to adjust his policies to suit this constituency. The result is that the very terms of discussion and argument, let alone policies and decisions, are circumscribed and defined by the interplay between responsible leaders and interested persons and groups who concern themselves with that area of the city's life.

However, despite the fact that these forces challenge each other and engage in constant conversation over decisions to be made affecting the city's population, this challenge is never sufficient. Let no one assume that an easy "balance of power" created between conflicting interests will produce a more humane social policy and result in an increase of justice among men. Even groups with conflicting points of view, when they concern themselves for a long period of time over issues in the same area of city life, develop a consensus and way of living with one another that itself needs to be challenged. They come more and more to represent themselves and the groups that support them; they think less and less of those who are unrepresented. The ease with which a minority political party can adapt to its chronic state of being out of power and seek favors from its opponents, the propensity of labor and management in many of the city's low-wage industries to sign "sweetheart contracts" that ensure the union of its position as bargaining agent in exchange for economic gain to the employer, the failure of groups representing the urban migrants of a previous generation to show concern for the problems of those who are coming into the cities today—these few examples should remind us that there are always those who are unrepresented or underrepresented.

Thus, the process of challenge and criticism is a constant one. Social idealists who assume that man's ability to imagine and to plan can bring into being the city that will last a millennium are doomed to be disappointed. The results of our best efforts to solve stubborn human problems prove to bring problems of their own as well as solutions to the situations we had in mind. Naïve voters who assume that the "outs" will settle everything when elected are also doomed to frustration. The "outs," upon assuming office, become those who are "in." And cynics who state confidently that nothing can be changed are also doomed to be wrong. Change is constant, and the protest that today seems a cloud smaller than a man's hand will tomorrow fill the heavens with portent and warning.

ANOTHER CASE HISTORY

No problem facing the American metropolis in these days is more urgent and more pervasive than the influence of racial discrimination on housing patterns. The center city of most metropolitan areas has been the place where one could find the substandard housing areas filled with members of minority groups—Negroes, rural whites, Mexicans, Puerto Ricans, Chinese, Japanese—the group varying from city to city. To some people this has seemed only a repetition of the classic pattern in American cities: the newcomers settling first in the city "ghetto," which serves as a port of entry, then moving to the outlying areas with the succeeding years. However, in the case of racial groups that have been the object of discrimination, the familiar pattern has undergone two drastic changes.

First, the proportion of nonwhite population in the center city of many metropolitan areas has been growing at a rate far exceeding the influx of these people into the city. The traditional ghetto areas, filled to overcrowding or displaced through urban renewal, have spilled over into surrounding neighborhoods or reproduced themselves in other older residential sections. All this has been happening, not at the time of the greatest influx of new population into the metropolitan area, but five, ten, and fifteen years later. Part of this dramatic change can be attributed to marriages and births among the younger migrants, leading to increased population. But a more potent factor has been the flight of older white residents from areas that begin to house nonwhites and members of minority groups. Increased numbers of nonwhite people in the city, then, are not the major reason for their growing share in the population of the center city. Prejudice and discrimination on the part of those who feel they have to leave the city is far more responsible for the situation.

Second, the outlying areas of the metropolis, while maintaining through the years a constant percentage of nonwhite residents, have been doing very little to absorb the increases resulting from migration and birth. In fact, when nonwhites have sought to move out and secure better housing, they have either been rebuffed or forced to pay higher prices for property in areas that rapidly become suburban ghettos. Thus, the outer parts of the urban region, at the same time they are tightening a ring of discrimination around the center city and preventing the exodus of nonwhite families who would like to share in suburban life, are also insisting that the city ghetto be reproduced for those who are fortunate enough to move.

These two trends now operate to defy all the best efforts of government and concerned citizens to eliminate ghettos. The metropolitan area could be a tweed pattern of block after block, community after community with Negro and white, majority and minority living side by side. Yet, the forces of racial discrimination that promote flight and prevent expansion combine to make it a checkerboard with overcrowded minority-group islands surrounded by territory into which they are forbidden to move. In some of the more populated areas of the country the trend has now extended so far from the center city that it seems only a matter of a few years until the white population fleeing contact with minorities in one metropolis is going to run past its counterpart fleeing from another city and come face to face once more with the very groups it seeks to shun. This is the price we are now paying for private prejudice against members of minority groups when it results in public patterns of discrimination in the field of housing.

Obviously a situation like this does not arise spontaneously, without knowledge or encouragement by the authorities of the city and those who sit in the pyramids of power. A closer look at the causes of residential discrimination will disclose that it is not created only by the prejudice of individual homeowners who sell their homes at the first approach of a minority group or who refuse to welcome them as neighbors. Real estate operators encourage panic selling so that they can buy cheap and sell dear; mortgage bankers ask a higher rate from the minority group member and blackball whole sections of the city for credit on real estate; city officials allow public expenditures for schools and other improvements to decrease in ghetto areas while they are concerned to furnish services to those in new housing sections; merchants and other businessmen look at the ghetto as the place to make a profit with cheap goods while considering the area dominated by those who discriminate as the place to make new investments. All these and many more have contributed their share to perpetuating the pattern of discrimination in housing, if they were not the ones who established it in the first place.

Few situations would seem to call out more insistently for an Amos to set God's plumb line down beside the actual life of men in the metropolitan area. But the individuals and groups offering criticism and challenge to the power of prejudice that has molded our present patterns of discrimination in housing are comparatively few and relatively weak. In a large city today nearly everyone favors tolerance and brotherhood. During February large groups of the city's elite and concerned gather at banquets, forums, lectures, and services to celebrate Brotherhood Month. The buses and television screens are full of advertisements proclaiming the virtues of brotherhood. Yet many of those who attend the brotherhood meetings and nod appreciatively at the brotherhood messages are the very ones who go home to sleep in a neighborhood protected by a wall of discrimination from the necessity of residential living in brotherhood. Time and again they are able to answer, "But we don't have any problem here," because they live in an area that has completely insulated itself from contact with members of minority groups, even when members of such groups have the financial ability to rent or buy homes there.

Challenge and criticism does come sometimes, but usually it comes from those most deeply affected, the members of minority groups themselves. An organization representing their interests publishes a graphic report describing the discrimination being practiced in the field of housing and presenting recommendations for improvement. Or a single citizen, determined that his family will have the benefit of decent housing and a mixed neighborhood, courageously buys a home in a previously all-white neighborhood, endures the usual period of coolness, occasionally faces open hostility and threats until his residency is assured and accepted. Both represent prophetic thrusts, although both come from the ones who are bearing the brunt of discrimination.

In some states and cities the challenge is coming from official commissions and committees that have been set up by law to ensure equal treatment in housing, among other fields. Such groups, usually operating in an advisory way or through voluntary compliance, have been given the official task of challenging and criticizing the status quo. They often feel as lonely as Amos in Bethel, yet they do have the right to criticize patterns of discrimination. In other places groups of citizens have banded together to urge their neighbors to sign "good neighbor pledges" that pledge them to accept all groups of people into their neighborhood. In situations where an atmosphere of panic selling has been created, still other groups have joined to post signs in front of their homes saying, THIS HOUSE NOT FOR SALE, thus proclaiming that they do not wish to join the flight from minority groups and add to the discrimination in housing.

God regards the situation of his people who live in the metropolitan area. "Are not two sparrows sold for a penny?" says Jesus. "And not one of them will fall to the ground without your Father's will." (Matt. 10:29.) If God knows and cares for sparrows, how much more will he care for the plight of men. "Fear not, therefore; you are of more value than many sparrows." (Matt. 10:31.) Through the challenge and criticism brought by his prophets, God is continually reminding the city's multitudes and its leaders that he expects them to offer full worship and service, that he expects them to live with the same justice and righteousness he himself possesses. Yet, if God cares for sparrows who fall and die through natural causes, we can be quite sure that he is equally concerned for the plight of those men and women, youth and children, who do not fall but are pushed by the pressure of human circumstance and decisions that others have made. The judgment of God sees farther and knows more wisely than any of our human efforts to secure justice.

Chapter IV

The City of Man and the City of God:
God and Social Reconstruction

THE ENGLISH LANGUAGE OBSCURES THE FACT THAT
"city," "citizen," and "civilization" all share a common
Latin root and represent different forms of the same basic
idea. City (*civitas*) is the total community to which men
belong. It is the place where they hold their citizenship
and feel the ties that bind them to their fellows. In the
ancient world one city could be a whole state; therefore,
the word was used interchangeably for city and state. In
the modern world a city must be counted to include all its
surrounding region, even though this is usually neither the
state nor the nation. Citizens (*cives*) are the inhabitants
of the city. They receive their citizenship through belong-
ing to the community and participating in its affairs, not
the other way around. Although we like to think it is the
citizens who come together to make the city, they really
receive their citizenship through their participation in the
city's life.

Civilization (from the Latin *civilis*) means that a
group of people have been brought to the state of being
citizens in the fullest sense. Although we often use the
term to refer to the culture or society of any group of
people, it should be saved for those forms of human culture which most fully realize the possibilities of human

society. A civilized community is a city that, through the development of art, science, religion, and government, has reached the point where its citizens can truly enjoy their citizenship.

Lewis Mumford points out in his history of the development of cities, *The City in History,* that the earliest reasons for the establishment of cities were not, as some imagine, the benefits that would be gained by the citizens. The walled fortress-city for the protection of its inhabitants and the city as a center of trade and commerce arose comparatively late in human history. The earliest cities were created for the benefit of divinity as burial places or as sanctuaries. Civilization, the process of coming together into cities for the advancement of human community, has depended from the start on men's acknowledgment of God, however weak or distorted that faith may have been. And we must add that the attainment of civilization still requires faith in the God who has made us for community and sets us to live in cities. The true city, the faithful citizen, the full civilization, will be known only when the Lord "will dwell with them, and they shall be his people, and God himself will be with them" (Rev. 21:3), because the dwelling of God is with men.

Two Cities or One?

The Christian hope teaches that one day men will know the blessedness of the city of God. When God is truly worshiped and served, man will share the harmony with his Heavenly Father and his human neighbor that the Creator intended from the beginning. But Christian thinkers have always found it difficult to determine whether we are dealing with two cities or one. Do we see an earthly city, the city of man, which must someday be replaced by a celestial city, the city of God? Or do we see only the metropolis itself that is gradually to be transformed into a perfect society, the city of God?

Augustine of Hippo, writing after the fall of Rome to the Goths in A.D. 410, was the first to propose that there are two cities here. Faced with the necessity of explaining why great Rome had fallen, even though her rulers were Christians, Augustine replied in his work, *The City of God,* that there were two cities, the earthly and the heavenly. The earthly city, the city of man, is formed by love of self and glories in itself; the heavenly city, the city of God, is formed by love of God and glories in the Lord. The barbarian invasion, said Augustine, had destroyed a part of the city of man, but the city of God was still to come. The Christians in Rome held citizenship in the city of God and remained faithful to that city, even under persecution, but they had not made Rome into the city of God. All that can be obtained in the earthly city is temporal peace, while the city of God will bestow an eternal peace that cannot be broken. Christian citizens of Rome, then, were but pilgrims journeying on to the celestial city.

Where Augustine saw two cities, the thinkers of the Enlightenment and the men who founded the United States of America felt there was basically one city, the city of this world which is being transformed through progress into the city of God. This vision of a completely new world to be secured according to "the Laws of Nature and of Nature's God" is implicit in the writings and utterances of the Founding Fathers. It is made quite explicit in the following stanza from Katherine Lee Bates's national hymn:

> O beautiful for patriot dream
>   That sees, beyond the years,
> Thine alabaster cities gleam,
>   Undimmed by human tears!

America! America!
    God shed his grace on thee,
And crown thy good with brotherhood
    From sea to shining sea.

The pilgrimage here is a shorter one from the Atlantic Ocean to the Pacific, from the founding of the Colonies to the time when the nation's cities will all conform to God's intention and become the city of God "undimmed by human tears."

In raising the question about how the city of God will come, we have set the alternatives against each other: Are there two cities here, or one? Yet, a more careful look at Scripture, at Augustine, at the thinkers of the Enlightenment, and at our own situation will show us that the alternatives are not necessarily exclusive of each other. For the Old Testament prophets the promise of a restored Jerusalem did not assume the complete absence of the Lord from the city before that time. In the New Testament, although the apostle Paul looked forward to the end when Christ "delivers the kingdom to God the Father after destroying every rule and every authority and power," he saw even in the present moment that God, through Christ, the "first fruits," "must reign until he has put all enemies under his feet" (I Cor. 15:22-28). Augustine clearly understood that the city of God is not all future but impinges on the life of the present in the lives of the faithful who already live according to a dual citizenship. And the apostles of reason in America, for all their confidence in the power of the people to establish a new order of the ages, were still concerned that their revolution should have "reasons which will justify it in the sight of God and man" (cf. letter of John Adams, July 3, 1776).

The only city that we seem to know in the present is the city of man, the city founded on self-love and erected to the glory of man. Yet we remember that God set man in human society for the worship of God and the achievement of true fellowship with his fellowmen. The city of God, the city founded on love of God and erected to his glory, still retains its essential skeleton in spite of the attempts of the architecture of sin to cover it over with walls of man's devising and to bedizen its interior with the grotesque decorations of pride and self-love and greed. We also remember that God has sent his Son for the redemption of mankind. Therefore, the grace of God allows, even in the midst of this time, some of the qualities of that future city to be realized within the life of our cities. Complete fulfillment and the perfected city of God will not come until the end; yet some of that divine order of redemption can be known even here and now.

THE REIGN OF CHRIST

If Christ had not come and men were still left in their sins, we could well afford to leave our discussion where it was at the close of the last chapter. God made the city to worship and serve him, but the city has rejected that service and turned aside to its own ways. God gave rulers to the city for the creation of order and the restraint of sin, but those who are in authority need the judgment of God's justice fully as much as those over whom they exercise their power. God intended the culture of man to praise him and to free all men for their God-given manhood, but "civilization" now can only mean that which is organized against God and seeks to exalt man and his works. In short, the city could then only be reminded of its original charter and the way in which that divine purpose has been violated. The city could only know God as its Creator and as its Judge.

As those who know the reign of Christ by God's grace through faith in his cross and resurrection, however, Christians cannot be content with the duties of obedience to the powers that be, and of challenge and criticism in the name of divine justice. They know God as Redeemer, and have a responsibility to bear witness to the new possibilities opened up for mankind through God's reconciling love. Righteousness and restored relationships are the marks of the reign of Christ in the life of the world. Even as physical healing marked the ministry of Jesus and the apostles, so social reconstruction and growth in civilization can be part of the healing ministry of Christ in this age. The message of reconciliation between God and man and between man and man is verified and demonstrated in power when reconciliation occurs in the life of the city. When the Seventy returned to Jesus, they came with joy, saying, " 'Lord, even the demons are subject to us in your name!' " To this Jesus replied, " 'I saw Satan fall like lightning from heaven' " (Luke 10:17–18). The process of social change in the metropolitan area can demonstrate the same power and proclaim the same conquest.

CHANGE AND RECONSTRUCTION

If there is a single constant factor to expect in the life of the metropolis, that factor is change. The great cities of Europe may pride themselves on their ancient buildings and historic monuments that have stood unchanged for centuries, but the cities of America are in constant flux. A comparison of street plans or skyline pictures will show that almost every American city differs drastically today from its appearance fifty years ago. The change is no less striking in forms of government, groups making up the population, types of commerce and industry, activities, and organizations. Social change is constant and occurs on all sides.

Although it is customary in the United States to assume that anything which is new or different represents progress, much of the change represents shifts in fashion or taste rather than basic improvement in the condition of the city's citizens. These changes are less than they seem, for they satisfy the desire of the city's residents for novelty and the need of the city's leaders for activity, yet they contribute little or nothing to the proclamation of the rule of Christ over the power of sin in the life of the metropolis.

Much is being said these days about the task of social reconstruction facing the citizens of the newly independent nations of Africa and Southeast Asia. With populations ranging from a few tens of thousands to millions, these states are finding it necessary to redirect the course of inherited institutions and to erect new structures so that their people may enjoy the benefits of politics, economics, health, education, family life, and other areas of the common life. The problems that must be solved in moving from political subservience to responsible independence are massive, yet in every land we hear of leaders, technicians, and simple citizens who welcome the challenge of social reconstruction. The changes to be made in the life of society will be deep-seated and far-reaching, for they will determine the future of the citizens of these new nations. Social reconstruction is an exciting and challenging task.

Yet, when we look at the life of any American metropolis, we see problems as complex and challenges as great as those facing any African or Asian nation. The number of people affected within a single metropolitan area may be many times the total population of one of the new members of the United Nations. If all those who depend on the city or cities at the heart of a metropolitan area are included, the satellite region covers hundreds of square miles. Within that territory are many towns and residential areas that did not exist fifteen years ago, and even in the older sections great segments of the population did not occupy their present place of residence at that time. The political structures and other mechanisms of planning and control are often as unsuited to the new problems and situations facing the region as were the British, French, or Dutch colonial administrations of recent memory. Surely here is a situation that cries out for reconstruction as deep-seated and far-reaching as in the new nations. Few recognize, however, that the basic need is for reconstruction, not ephemeral change.

One of the reasons for this blindness is the newness of urbanism as a way of life, even for the United States. In 1800 no city in the Western World had a population of a million. London had just a little less than that number, Paris was a little over half a million, whereas in America Philadelphia led with a population of 69,403, followed by New York with 60,489. Chicago, Detroit, and Los Angeles had not yet been settled. By 1900 three American cities held more than a million persons, and the census of 1960 showed five cities exceeding this figure. However, whereas ten years earlier 15 cities were over a half a million, 21 cities topped that figure in 1960, and 130 had populations of 100,000 or more compared with 107 in 1950. Estimates indicate that close to 70 percent of our people live in metropolitan areas.

The very rapidity of this growth has meant that city life had come into existence and we were living with it before we felt the necessity to prepare for its coming. The growth of central cities has taken place within two generations; the suburban explosion has occurred in the last two decades. Every indication points to more of the same in the future. Homer Hoyt, in a study for the Urban Land Institute, has predicted that the world's urban population will triple in the next forty years to 3,416,000,000, so that more than half the world's population will live in cities by the year 2000. The problems of urbanism are hard upon us, and no city in our country has more than two generations of experience on which to draw for guidance.

Another reason for blindness to the need for social reconstruction is the pattern of control that exists in every metropolitan region. The reins of political, economic, and social power are in the hands of those who were newcomers to the area in a previous generation. In New York those of Irish, Italian, and Eastern European origin dominate the city's life at the very time when Negroes and Puerto Ricans are ceasing to be minorities and coming to make up a substantial segment of the population. On the West Coast, in the sprawling vastness of Los Angeles, earlier settlers from the Middle West hold control, although the greatest influx includes whites and Negroes from the South and Southwest, along with Mexican Americans. The same situation prevails across the land. Leaders representing the desire of older residents to retain their hard-won gains and continue in positions of control sit at the top of the pyramids of power. Although these groups desire a continuation of those changes that consolidate their dominance, they are wary of reconstruction that might admit others to a share in social leadership.

Still another cause of this blindness is the "suburban" mentality itself. Most families have moved to the outlying sections of the metropolitan area "for the sake of the children," as they put it. By this they mean they went seeking newer homes, less-crowded neighborhoods, better schools, more green areas and playgrounds, and higher social prestige. The very act of moving shows rejection of the city and the notion that their family should live as part of the larger society of the metropolitan area.

Yet, the inhabitants of the suburbs are no less a part of the city when they sleep on its outskirts than when they looked out their bedroom windows at its pavements and buildings. In spite of their wish to busy themselves with the "small-town" problems of their local village, school district, or tax area, the metropolitan difficulties they seek to flee are still part of their own situation. Road construction, traffic control, and rapid transit are often more gall-ing to the suburbanite who must travel everywhere by car, bus, or train and must permit trucks to travel through his boundaries than to the resident of the central city. The employee who works in the city and leaves every evening to sleep outside its limits often has a larger share of his Federal, state, and local taxes going to the support of the residents of the city than to the place where he and his family dwell.

In spite of this involvement, however, the "suburban" mentality resents the continued claim of urban problems for attention and seeks to reject any responsibility for the work of social reconstruction in the metropolitan area. Like the older residents of newly expanded towns who vote against school bond issues because their own children are grown, the suburbanites—who oppose that kind of unconcern when directed at their needs—turn around and deny that they share the burden of the needs of others in the metropolitan region.

The Need for Metropolitan Strategy

On the American continent great cities have been with us for less than a century, and the sprawling, exploding metropolis for less than two decades. Almost all the changes that have occurred are reactions to the unstruc-tured flow of people from other lands to ours and from the rural areas to the cities. The unprecedented growth in the use of the private automobile, the spread of radio and television, the multiplication of labor-saving devices and automation both in the home and at work—these have created changes to which cities are still responding. In almost every case, moreover, the changes were well under way before the city's leaders began to devise means to deal with them. And many times the symptoms of change have received far more attention than the underlying causes.

When one considers some of the special services required, the picture becomes even more complex. Public works, water supply, garbage disposal, fire protection, police, courts, public health, traffic control and safety, recreation, air pollution control, noise abatement, education, fiscal policy and taxation, housing, redevelopment, city planning, rapid transit, welfare services—all these are important to the proper functioning of a metropolitan area, and all impinge directly on the life of the citizens. Each requires its own encyclopedia of specialized knowledge and is presided over by its own hierarchy of technicians. But each of these specialized groups is usually more concerned with the tactics necessary to solve its own limited set of problems than with the wider strategy required for genuine social reconstruction.

The deepest need of every metropolitan area is for a coherent strategy that can weld together the complex, competing forces that seek to make segments of the city's life over into their own image. Such a strategy requires an ability to see the whole in the midst of all its parts. Where each segment of the metropolitan power structure seems most interested in securing its own share of the available resources and recognition, some groups need to be developing strategy that will take these into consideration while looking beyond them to the common good. The late mayor of New York, Fiorello H. LaGuardia, has already become an urban legend because he raced to fires and scenes of disturbance, read the comics over the radio during a newspaper strike, and gave marketing tips to housewives. But his abiding concern for the minutiae of municipal life and the daily concerns of the citizens was founded upon an ability to picture the whole city and take every New Yorker into account. This sort of vision is needed in every metropolitan area today.

A metropolitan strategy also requires an ability to see the future in the midst of the present. No one can predict all the trends of so dynamic a society as the one in which we live. Yet it is still possible to see the direction in which much of the present is pointing. Although those involved in each of the pyramids of power seem most interested in present advantage, some groups need to be looking beyond the city that already is to the city that is in the state of becoming. Philadelphians still have reason to thank William Penn for the four small squares he laid out at the corners of his plan, tiny oases of light and air surrounded by the urban hurly-burly. And Chicagoans of a future date will give similar thanks to those who provided for the belts of forest preserves in Cook County that will retain natural areas for recreation and water supply when the expanding metropolis has pushed its limits far beyond them. Our vision cannot be bounded by the present.

Finally, a metropolitan strategy will require an ability to determine those times and places where leadership is needed. Since most crucial decisions in the metropolitan area involve a long period of discussion and the achievement of an informal or formal consensus before policy is set and action can be taken, they do not result in concrete projects until long after the need arises. Accommodation, negotiation, and compromise are used to secure a working unanimity, but these are slow processes. Therefore, there is always need for those who can discern the issues and begin to raise them, so that the powers that be will start mobilizing their forces to meet them. Although the innovators are bound to be labeled "controversial," time and again they prove to be the watchmen on the wall alerting the body politic to its responsibilities.

The natural inertia and self-interest of those who possess influence are bound to be thrown on the side of keeping things the way they are. The pressure to eschew the work of reconstruction and maintain the status quo, even in the face of radical challenge and change, is communicated in various ways: fear among the leaders who face loss of their own positions, pessimism among the technicians who have seen their careful proposals resisted and struck down time after time, silence and apathy among the people at large who have come to expect that "nothing can be done." Yet, in spite of these pressures to conformity and inertia, there is always more plasticity in the situation than many recognize.

A simple household worker was arrested for sitting in the front of a segregated bus in Montgomery, Alabama, and a broad-gauged challenge to traditional patterns of race relations in that city was launched. A newspaper kept asking questions about the conduct of the police force in Chicago, and a complete housecleaning of the department was finally instituted. Alcoa and U.S. Steel, with corporate headquarters in Pittsburgh, resisted the pull to locate the center of their operations in New York's Wall Street, and the renaissance of Pittsburgh's Golden Triangle was ensured by their decisions to build new office buildings there. The examples could be multiplied indefinitely, but they demonstrate that, when the need for leadership is recognized, there are always times and places calling for its exercise.

ONE MORE CASE HISTORY

Few urban problems gain more attention with less understanding than those of troubled youth, popularly labeled "juvenile delinquency." In every city a whole raft of charitable organizations, the school system, the police department, juvenile courts, recreational facilities, and family services all gain support for their activities with youth on the basis of "preventing juvenile delinquency." Each undoubtedly provides necessary services to youth and deals with part of the picture. Yet, in spite of the best efforts of all concerned, rates of juvenile misbehavior and the seriousness of the crimes committed by minors have continued to increase steadily since the end of World War II.

One urban neighborhood, faced with recurring acts of violence by teen-age gangs that claimed to be organized for self-protection, but insisted on waging preventive wars, responded first with indignation at mass meetings, calls for more police protection and special youth workers, and attempts to provide increased recreation and athletics. In the course of working together, all the agencies and concerned citizens began to find that, important though their own role might be, it did not result in decreased violence unless carried out in conscious cooperation and coordination with the work of others. As time went on, their efforts were concentrated first on the gang leaders, then on their followers, and finally on younger brothers and sisters who were set to follow in their footsteps. The tactics of dealing with specific outbreaks of violence began in time to yield to the strategy of dealing with youth as a whole. What had been "rumbles committees" trying to keep track of the warring contingents became "youth service teams" devoted to seeing that all who were concerned about youth worked together effectively.

Even this did not prove to be sufficient, however, as it became more and more evident that much of the misbehavior was the result of the failure of urban society to have a real place for working-class youth. The schools did not talk their language and were not preparing them for the real choices open to them in society. Social agencies could offer them a "good time" and concerned adult leaders, but they were not providing a sense of worth for their activities. Probation officers, family service workers, school guidance personnel, mental health therapists, could talk over problems with them and their families, but they could promise no relief from the stigma of being poor or outcasts in the city. Plans for support, guidance, and activity were all helpful, yet they all fell short of the root-and-branch reconstruction necessary to provide these young people with the opportunities necessary for their growth to healthy adulthood.

A broader strategy was necessary. Because many were not trained or ready to accept even the most menial jobs and were prevented by patterns of discrimination and union restrictions from gaining rudimentary experience, the whole field of employment became a major focus. Special centers for the counseling and placement of youth, pre-employment training and subsidized work have been planned. Because many were becoming school dropouts and many more were just going through the motions, the field of education also received attention. Remedial reading classes, curriculum materials that use experiences familiar in their daily lives, increased individual guidance and cultural enrichment, are to be provided in the public schools. And because the hostility and alienation which was acted out in teen-age gang warfare often had its roots in the hostile attitudes and feeling of alienation on the part of adults, the integration of all groups into the community and the overcoming of passivity and despair became essential. Neighborhood councils to furnish a focus for constructive action and special programs to reach those who feel shut out of community affairs will be organized. None of these programs by itself provides a panacea for the displacement of youth in an urban neighborhood; but, taken together, they provide a wider strategy around which all available resources can be mobilized for the necessary work of social reconstruction.

RELEVANCE OF THE CHRISTIAN HOPE

One of the most discouraging discoveries of those who have been working with the problem of teen-age violence has been the fact that, when open warfare was averted and the gang groups began to break up, many of those who had been most involved shifted to the use of narcotics and became addicts. One form of social sin had merely been replaced by another. Few problems in urban life have proven as hopeless and as resistant to cure as that of narcotics addiction. Once "hooked," the addict seems powerless to keep from returning to his habit, no matter how many times he may go through withdrawal from the use of drugs.

In New York City, where the rate of addiction has been the highest in the United States, it has been primarily groups organized by Protestant churches that have been willing to bear the stigma of association with addicts when possession of drugs was a crime, and to stick with the addict and his family over the endless periods that precede and follow each attempt to "kick the habit." Faithful to God, "who did not spare his own Son but gave him up for us all" (Rom. 8:32), and trusting in the power of the cross to deliver from all sin, these churches have refused to count the addict as hopeless or to confine the work of social reconstruction to those situations which respond most quickly to our human strategies.

Because the resistance of sin, both in persons and in the city at large, is so strong, the Christian hope possesses a relevance that surpasses any simple social optimism. Knowing that the power of sin has been broken in Christ, yet realizing that the complete fulfillment of the city of God has not yet been reached, the Christian is able to plan and to labor in hope. His hope is founded not on his own efforts nor on the efficacy of his strategies and plans, no matter how carefully drawn. Ultimately his hope is based on the power of God to redeem a broken and disobedient creation, to realize within the life of the metropolitan area some of the life of the city of God.

Chapter V

What Can the Church Do?

GOD AND THE CITY

THE CITY LIVES ITS LIFE UNDER THE RULE OF GOD. Even the mightiest metropolis cannot escape the sway of this omnipotent Lord. Even the haughtiest leader perched high atop one of the pyramids of power cannot avoid the inexorable judgments of the God of justice, mercy, and peace. And even the humblest victim of unfortunate circumstance or the ill-will of others cannot be denied the comforts of the God of love, who sent his own Son for the salvation of sinners. Our minds are overwhelmed when we are confronted by the magnitude and diversity of human life within a metropolitan area. It is almost impossible to see the city or its people whole. Yet, we are reminded that God is the Lord of the city, and that he sees it in all its magnitude and diversity at the same time that he stoops in concern for its smallest part.

The central argument of this book has been that the city cannot overlook and deny the rule of God, even though it does ignore the Christian church. God is the one who made the city. As its Creator, he has provided the powers that be to keep order and to allow the freedom that permits each man to make his own contribution to the common life. Neither can the city ignore the fact that its sins are called to account by the perfect justice of God. As its Judge, God has provided prophets who, by their challenge and criticism, raise continuous questions about the nature of the city's worship and service.

Above all, the city needs to know that its redemption has come. Through the reign of Christ the power of sin is already being broken and wholeness is being restored to the Babel of metropolitan life. As the Redeemer who gives the city of God to men and dwells in its midst, God works out his salvation in the world as we know it. Through the processes of social change and social reconstruction, he is making it possible for men to appreciate the dimensions of their eternal citizenship and to lay hold on the fruits of civilization. The overwhelming power and goodness of God's love in Christ means that the words of the prophet Isaiah are already being fulfilled:

The Spirit of the Lord is upon me,
because he has anointed me to preach good news to the poor.
He has sent me to proclaim release to the captives
and recovering of sight to the blind,
to set at liberty those who are oppressed,
to proclaim the acceptable year of the Lord.

(Isa. 61:1–2 as quoted in Luke 4:18–19.)

The city's Creator and Judge is also the city's Redeemer, and its multitudes are called to repent and believe in his Son, Jesus Christ.

THE CHURCH AND THE CITY

"Religion is a private matter between me and God," says the average church member. By this very statement he has shut his eyes to the fact that God is at work in the fellowship of the church and in the wider life of the city. "The church is supposed to be in but not of the world," adds a more sophisticated Protestant. But the manner in which he puts the proposition places emphasis on the church's separation from the life of the world around it and forgets that Christ sent his disciples "into the world" (cf. John 17:15–18). "The church I'm looking for is the one where I can feel at home," states another typical Protestant. Yet the result of seeking to satisfy the desires of its members and provide a separate home for every segment of the city's diverse population has been to make the urban church virtually indistinguishable from its surroundings.

For almost a century American Protestants have been intensely concerned about the life of urban populations. City mission work, founded to bring the gospel to unchurched masses, and the Social Gospel movement, intended to express the implications of that gospel for society, were both part of the response to the growth of cities in America. However, the net result of years of dedicated effort has been the creation of a few isolated islands of urban churchmanship in the midst of a widening sea of popular indifference and institutional flight. Having built its house on the sand of private preference, social aloofness, and cultural conformity, Protestantism in metropolitan areas has seen its influence steadily decline.

But a deeper problem than this loss of relevance has been the fact that, while claiming to be the place where God is known most truly, the churches have actually been as far from their Lord as the rest of the city's population —if not farther. Looking for God's presence only within their own walls, the church has neglected the clear evidence of his work in the miles and miles of streets and highways that stretch on every side. Expecting that the Almighty will do his most important work through its members, the church has overlooked the service of his ministers in the common life, the leaders of the city. Seeking like-mindedness and an easy cultural unity within the fellowship of the local congregation, churches have ignored the overwhelming diversity that God has brought together within the metropolitan area with ever-varying bonds of relationship. Surely, God has not deserted his people in our cities, but the churches that claim to serve in his name may have deserted him.

GOD AND THE CHURCH

God is greater than his church, and the glories of his salvation far exceed the church's ability to represent and embody that salvation. Paul Tillich has called this understanding of the relation between God and his church "the Protestant principle," because it first became clear to Christians when Martin Luther, John Calvin, and the other Reformers insisted that the church itself, like every man, was bound to the guidance of the Word of God and stood under its judgment.

The Protestant principle helps us to view the church in its proper relation to God. First, the church, like every other human agency, lives under the judgment of its Redeemer and Lord. Like every other individual, institution, and group in the metropolis, the churches are held responsible to God. Whenever the churches try to claim too much for themselves, they need to be reminded that they possess an institutional life which interacts with the other parts of the life of the metropolis. Religious life, although far from possessing the largest measure of power, itself occupies one of the seats of power. Therefore, the churches cannot escape the judgment of God's plumb line of justice nor the claims of God's redemption. When we see churches in the outlying suburbs of the metropolis contributing to the general feeling of escape from and irresponsibility toward the problems of the wider city, we should recognize that they too have strayed from their God. And when we see churches in city neighborhoods acquiescing in the general feeling that "You can't fight city hall" and "Things are bound to get worse," we should acknowledge that they have lost sight of the reality of God's salvation.

Second, the Protestant principle teaches that God can work out his purposes in spite of the churches and beyond the churches, as well as through them. The church as a people of God has been called into being to "declare the wonderful deeds of him who called you out of darkness into his marvelous light" (I Peter 2:9). So long as the church remains true to this calling, the grace that has given it life continues to flow through its members and communicate life to the culture around it. But, when the church no longer declares the deeds of its Savior and Lord, and loses its concern for their impact on others, God does not leave men comfortless. He raises up out of the life of the age (Lat. *saeculum*) "secular" ministers who bear witness to his power as the city's Creator, the Judge of metropolitan life, and the Redeemer of the urban multitudes. Indeed, he already supplements the work of the churches with other evidences of his illimitable grace. It is a sad commentary on the churches' understanding of themselves and God's work that they so often credit God with doing only through them what he manifestly is also doing through others. Time and again the churches of the inner city have given great amounts of time and energy to programs of recreation, group fellowship, and guidance for troubled and displaced youth. All around them other agencies—some of them voluntary groups working in the name of philanthropy and community betterment, some of them governmental agencies working in the name of law and order, and social health—are carrying on similar work. Yet, in a display of colossal arrogance, the churches will often claim the exclusive blessing of God's grace upon their own labors, when he clearly is granting fruits to the efforts of others.

Thus, the church is called upon to assume a proper understanding of its relation to God and to the world.

God calls the church into being as a fellowship that, living in faith, hope, and love, is to bear witness to his wonderful deeds that lie all around the citizens of the metropolitan area. The Lord does not promise that he will accomplish all his purposes through the church, but he clearly expects this people to recognize him and acknowledge his work. Yet, the church is not always faithful to its calling. Also, the church sees that the powers that be and all who share in the life of the metropolis have been bounded by the grace of God. The reign of Christ has begun to exert its power not only upon those who bear Christ's name, but also upon the whole life of the world. No corner of the city's life, no matter how small or hidden, can escape his sway. But we know full well that the church's members have yet to reach into every corner of the vast metropolis.

The Church's Ministry

The eye of a television camera is trained upon the metropolitan area, seeking out a dramatic example of the church's concern for those who dwell there. What does the camera eye usually find? An ordained clergyman (identified by his backwards collar) walking the dark streets and serving the inhabitants by bearing the cross of suffering and sharing the victory of redemption. This, says the electronic informant to millions of viewers, is the church's ministry. And the unseen audience is confirmed in its assumption that the church's ministry is carried on by its professionals—the pastors, the priests, the missionaries, the special church workers. Even members of the Christian fellowship share this misunderstanding that the work of the church is either done by the clergy or else assumed by lay people in order to "help the clergy out."

In truth, the church's ministry is the responsibility of the whole people of God. Every member of a Christian church is a minister to whom has been committed the difficult work of bearing witness to his Lord. Jesus was speaking of this witness when he addressed his disciples in the Sermon on the Mount:

You are the light of the world. A city set on a hill cannot be hid. Nor do men light a lamp and put it under a bushel, but on a stand, and it gives light to all in the house. Let your light so shine before men, that they may see your good works and give glory to your Father who is in heaven. (Matt. 5: 14–16.)

The witness of the Christian man is not hidden, private, secret. Like a town set high on a hill where it can command the valleys all around it, like a lamp that must be put where it can throw its light into every corner, the fellowship of the Christian church cannot hide or obscure its witness. "You are the light of the world," said Jesus; but light that is hidden or kept low or turned off does not benefit anyone.

The church bears its witness in many ways in the midst of the metropolitan area. The very existence of houses of worship, often occupying sites that would be extremely valuable if they were developed commercially, can be a sign that the service of God is a part of the city's high calling. Far more important than the buildings, however, is the worship that is carried on within their walls. Outside the church as it worships is the broken urban world, while inside a faithful congregation listens to the word of God proclaimed and interpreted, and receives in faith the broken body and poured-out blood of the world's Savior. God's grace is celebrated, remembered, and shown in the place where it is needed. The Lord is not forgotten, even among the multitudes of the metropolis. This is the witness of the church's worship.

The work of teaching borne by the church's members

is another part of its witness. Every family that raises its children to call upon the name of the Lord and to recognize the signs of his faithfulness and mercy in the busy hubbub that crowds the city's day increases the number of witnesses. Great portions of the church's time, energy, and financial resources are spent in the task of Christian education, education intended to multiply and deepen the knowledge of God in the metropolitan region. Not that the simple repetition of Biblical formulas will suffice. The cultural diversity of urban life forces church members to live every minute of their lives in the knowledge that many people do not believe as they do. In addition, the Christian's knowledge of his faith, of himself, and of the one to whom he tries to speak is often so faulty that his message is not heard, even though it is all-important for the life of men in the city. Yet, feeble though his attempts may be, the Christian's witness as he tries to teach others can help the multitudes know that even the most self-sufficient have a Creator, a Judge, a Redeemer, a Lord. This is the witness of the church's teaching.

When members of the church assist one another and move out to give service to the needs of the world, they are also bearing witness. The fabric of the city's life as a social organism, a way of living together, is strengthened and enriched by the ties binding Christians to one another in the fellowship of the church and binding them to their neighbors through the ministry of service. When church members stop in daily to check on an aged member who lives alone in a sparsely furnished room, or when they take time to lead a group in their neighborhood, such as Scouts, a boys' or girls' club, or an athletic team, they are not only being faithful to their Lord's pattern of service to human need. They are also, in the words of the Communion service, "proclaiming the Lord's death until he comes" (I Cor. 11:26). By their willingness to enter into another person's situation and share in his suffering,

Christians proclaim their willingness to bear the cross of the world, which is the cross of their Lord, in the power of his resurrection.

LIFE IN THE WORLD

None of these ministries can be performed by preachers alone. Only the whole Christian fellowship, every member of the church, can bear witness to the greatness of God, who holds the whole metropolitan area under his sway. Unless the major share of the ministry is borne by the laity, the ministry of the church in the city will be weak indeed. Jesus is reported as saying ,"Go into all the world and preach the gospel to the whole creation" (Mark 16:15). (Note that the Revised Standard Version places this passage in a footnote, because it is found only in some of the texts and versions.) If the church is defined in terms of its people, not its building, then the church is present at some time or other in every nook and cranny of the city. There is not a building into which the church has not entered—in the person of its members; there is hardly a household that has not felt the influence of a Christian; there is no structure of the city's social life, even the structures of power, in which members of the body of Christ are not involved or play no part.

However, the fact that the church lives most of its life in the world is still largely unrecognized. This explains why it is so hard to see the church's people when we look closely at the urban scene. They live on every city block, work in every office building, belong to almost every organization, vote in every election. Yet, they have failed to see that they are Christ's ministers within the metropolitan region. In fact, they have often been among those who have turned in horror from the complexities of the city's problems and its sinful neglect of proper worship to God. Repelled by the overwhelming task facing those who seek to maintain or criticize or reconstruct the *status quo,* they have neglected the very ministry to which they were called by Christ—preaching the gospel to *the whole creation.* Unlike Jesus, who himself ate with tax collectors and sinners, the churches gathered in his name refuse to acknowledge that God's redeeming love is sufficient for the multitudes of the metropolis.

Some churches in America's cities are beginning to recover the power of their Lord's command. Turning from a concept of mission that would see their main task to be filling the pews of the sanctuary on Sunday or crowding the building with activity every day of the week, they have called their members to the realization that the church's main ministry is carried on in the world, in the life of every day, in that which finds its focus outside the walls of the meetinghouse. The Christian is being helped to see that his daily work, no matter how prosaic or humble, is a part of his worship to God. The janitor and school teacher, the bank executive and factory worker, the postal employee and housewife—each in his own way shares in the God-given task of creating community through the *status quo;* each in his own way bears a portion of God's judgment upon the powers that be through challenge and criticism; each in his own way responds to God's redemption of the world in Christ as he takes part in the task of social reconstruction. The daily work of the church's members is a part of its ministry.

The whole life of the metropolitan region, not just those areas in which people earn their living, requires the ministry of Christians. For this reason, churches now are calling upon their members to accept at least one position of responsibility in the life of the community, such as working in at least one community organization as a part of their obedience to Christ. The volunteer who gives time to handicapped children, the mother and father who faithfully attend parents' meetings at the school on behalf of other children as well as their own, the worker who accepts the unwelcome task of shop steward, are all increasing the church's ministry within the life of the world. They can carry on such a ministry only if they recognize that it is a service to the Lord, but many churches are now equipping them for this through Bible-study groups, church school classes, special discussions, or vocational groups. The church must give up its claim to some of their time for the round of activities carried on by the fellowship inside its own building, but the Christian community gains through this multiplication and extension of its own work in the places where people are.

In defiance of the cliché, "Religion and politics do not mix," some urban churches have recognized that the basic decisions about the life of people in the city are made in the pyramids of power, especially those of business and politics. Members who already bear authority in these spheres are being reminded of their special responsibility for the metropolitan area. Instead of using the influence of the city's leaders for the material advancement of the church as an institution, these churches are challenging those leaders to exert that same influence for the renewal of the region and its people.

Not all churches have such highly placed persons in their fellowship; yet some are recognizing that in the American system of government every citizen can take a share in politics. For this reason, church members in these churches are being urged to participate in the political life of their city as a part of their ministry in Christ's name. Eschewing the crusade approach that would descend upon the city's political parties as the knight in shining armor determined to rescue the urban maiden from the toils of the politicians, these Christians have studied carefully the political structure of their area, chosen their party, and then moved into it at the local level of precinct or election district, where the basic work of political organization is done. Their chance to have a share in political decisions, then, comes as a natural result of their participation. And they find that the longer they work and play their part, the more influence they are able to wield and the higher up they move in the political structure. By laying claim to politics as a sphere of Christian ministry, they show that they are not content with the present situation where the churches are expected to leave business to the businessmen and politics to the politicians. They also demonstrate that the work of God can be done through politics as through all the other spheres of city life.

THE CHURCH AS AN INSTITUTION

Although it is primarily a fellowship of God's people bearing witness to his work and carrying on Christ's ministry in the world, the church is also an institution in the society of which it is a part. The religious pyramid of power in the metropolitan area is composed of all the religious groups, Protestant, Roman Catholic, Jewish. Existing within the framework set by the policies of business and government leaders, the institution of the church cannot avoid interaction with the other institutions. Its officials and administrators, concerned for the preservation and development of the institution, often contribute to the carving out of a "religious" sphere of life within the wider life of the city. Yet, in this very act they are denying that God is Lord of the metropolitan area as well as of its religious institutions. The same denial can be seen wherever a local congregation, concerned for its institutional self-preservation, retreats within its own walls and round of activities in the name of "religion" and being "spiritual."

The truth of the matter is that the institutional life of the church is a necessary part of its existence. No social organism can come into being without taking some form as an institution in society. The task of the Christian fellowship is not to deny its institutional nature but to see that this, like the life of the Christian, is used to bear witness to God's rule and judgment and loving grace. Like its members, the institution itself must live its life in the world as a service to its Lord.

In a suburban community the metropolitan area community drive asks that representatives of the churches sit on its board; the church as an institution needs to be represented. In a depressed neighborhood the improvement council asks that a local congregation become a member; the church as an institution needs to participate. In the city the mayor calls for a council of churches to name people for his committee on youth conservation; the church as an institution needs to show that this is part of its concern. The leaders of the metropolis are often ignorant of the church's concern for its life because they fail to see the church as an institution moving out of its own walls and getting involved in the issues that most deeply trouble the citizens. Every way that the churches find to bring their institutional life into the arena of civic life may open the way for criticism and opposition to their viewpoint, but it will also multiply their opportunities to be involved in the work that God is already doing in the city.

In some cases local congregations have gone one step farther and have placed themselves officially on record as a church on issues that affect the life of their community or the city as a whole. A zoning ordinance, an antidiscrimination law, a school budget, an administrative order within the welfare department, can all be opportunities for the church as an institution to make its voice heard. Each time such decisions are made, they are made with respect for all opinions within the fellowship and the widest possible agreement. However, like other acts of the congregation's life, they cannot wait for complete unanimity. In whatever way churches make plain that they share a concern for the total life of men and women in the city, it is clear that this ministry cannot be left wholly to the individual lives of the members. The institutional life of the church itself must also be lived in the world.

A Fellowship Without Boundaries

Each local congregation within the wider metropolis is tempted to think of its life and work as being limited to the geographical area in which the church's building is placed. Over and over again you hear churches commended because they "serve their community." In the sense that they do not remain within their own fellowship but become involved in the life of the world, such churches are being faithful to the church's mission. However, service to a particular locality is not enough in present-day metropolitan areas. Indeed, it can lead to neglect and denial of the larger community of which the church's members are a part.

Within the entire region surrounding a large city today are hundreds of separate communities, each sustained by the illusion that its problems are substantially different from those of the other inhabitants of the area. Within the city itself are dozens of neighborhoods feeding on the same illusion. To be sure, each locality has its own particular situation and its own peculiar history. Yet, no place is so isolated from the rest of the metropolitan area that it can afford the luxury of denying the great issues that face them all. "Service to our community," if it means nourishing the fallacy of localism, can also be a way of denying the church's essential ministry.

The Christian church is called to be a fellowship without boundaries. One local congregation may be wholly composed of people who live in a decayed low-income area, and another may have in its membership only those who live in expensive homes. This does not mean that the Christian church is low-income or high-income. One congregation may be all white and another all Negro. This does not mean that the Christian church is restricted to members of a single racial group. One congregation may worship in a large downtown edifice on the city's central square, and another may use a century-old building still sitting in the middle of farmland miles from the main business district. This does not mean that the Christian church lives only at the hub or on the rim of the metropolitan area.

Concern for the ministry of the local church in recent years has overshadowed the fact that the Christian church in urban areas cannot and should not be restricted to the congregation. Denominational judicatories and councils of churches are absolutely necessary if the full witness of the church is to be made. No local congregation can include in its membership all the areas of the city's life. Like the separate localities in the metropolis, individual congregations can lose sight of the larger picture of Christian fellowship without boundaries by giving too exclusive attention to local problems. In addition, the institutional impact of bodies that speak for groups of churches within the city is far greater than that made by any single congregation.

In this century of jet travel and world interdependence, the boundaries of the city do not stop at the point where population thins out and the countryside seems to take over. Within the nation there is talk of great "strip cities" that cover far wider areas and of the interrelated problems of all the metropolitan regions. The impact of world trade and finance on every city is so great that we must think of its problems in international as well as national terms. But the boundaries of the Christian fellowship do not stop at the edge of the metropolis or even at the continental limits. The church of Jesus Christ is a world fellowship: this is the testimony of national denominations and the National Council of Churches, of world confessional bodies and the World Council of Churches. Unless urban Christians are willing to face the problems of their local situation within this fellowship which is as wide as the world is wide, they will neither be taking true account of their actual situation nor bringing to it the full resources of the Christian family.

ABOUNDING IN HOPE

The Christian church is set in the world to be a witness to the work of God in the midst of the city of man. Although the tasks to which church members are called in relation to the power structure of urban society are no different from those required of every citizen, Christians perceive a different dimension in those tasks. They know it is God who made the powers that be, and therefore they are called to give more loyal attention to the requirements of community within the impersonality of the city's life. They recognize that it is God who measures the broken life of the city by his righteousness and justice, and therefore they are asked to respond more openly to challenge and criticism of the status quo. And above all, they bear witness to God's work of salvation in Christ that has overcome sin and is engaged in subduing the powers of sin that still remain. As those who live under the reign of the Lord Christ, Christians have more reason than any to seek the social reconstruction of the metropolitan area.

Responding to God in the life of the city can be a powerful witness to the gospel of Christ. In this sense, everything which church members do demonstrates whether or not they believe Jesus Christ is Lord and Savior. Founded in faith and strengthened by love, the Christian fellowship places its hope in a different place than do those persons who work alongside the church in the metropolitan area. Knowing that its work is God's work and that he alone can redeem, the church is set free from looking to immediate results for its final justification. As it takes its place among the power structures of the city, yet also identifies its life with those who must live under authority, the church of Jesus Christ abounds in hope. It goes to its work with this benediction:

May the God of hope fill you with all joy and peace in believing, so that by the power of the Holy Spirit you may abound in hope. (Rom. 15:13.)

Without the power of God given to it by the Holy Spirit, the church's work would be hopeless; with the power of the Holy Spirit, its work is abounding in hope.

Questions for Study and Discussion

Chapter I. Who Decides?

1. What is the difference between a "city" and a "metropolitan area"?

2. What place does geography play in the pattern made by a city on the landscape?

3. If the variety of life in a city is immediately caused by the will of man, what relation does it have to the will of God?

4. Give examples of ways in which tradition and precedent shape the life of a city.

5. Why does the newspaper reader only seem to have knowledge of how the decisions are made in a metropolitan area?

6. Do you agree with the observation that the "power elite," a few decision makers, primarily in business and government, set the basic framework for a city's life?

7. Business, government, education, organized labor, the professions, civic associations, welfare organizations, cultural groups, and religious institutions are the major pyramids of the metropolis. Can you describe their interaction in your own metropolitan area? Do you share the feeling that "they" control city life?

8. Examine closely one important decision being made in the life of your community. Do you find that complexity and compartmentalization are part of the picture? Who, in the last analysis, will make the decision?

9. "The whole institution of the church as a part of society is peripheral to the mainstream of the city's life." Do you agree or disagree with this statement?

Chapter II. The Powers That Be

1. What leads people to feel that a city is man's creation set over against God's creation in nature?

2. When Paul spoke of "the governing authorities," whom did he mean? In what sense can we speak of those involved in the power structure as "servants" or "ministers" of God?

3. What is the difference between official and unofficial power?

4. Is it possible to make a complete separation between law and gospel, or does the status quo exist for more than the restraint of sin?

5. How is it possible for virtual anarchy to result from the efforts of contending authorities to establish order?

6. Why do city problems go beyond the city limits, when city government does not?

7. What are the relative roles played in metropolitan regions today by city government, the surrounding metropolitan region, state government, and the Federal Government?

8. How does a slum get that way? What is required to create community there?

9. Study the effect of city planning upon your community. How are the relative claims of present community and future community decided?

Chapter III. Prophesying at Bethel

1. How does the judgment of God affect the life of a city?

2. Why are the sins of the city's leaders of particular interest to God?

3. Are men accountable for sins "known fully to God alone"?

4. Where would Amos go in a contemporary metropolitan area if he wished to "prophesy at Bethel"?

5. What is the relation of God's righteousness to the justice expected in human society?

6. In what sense can those who bring challenge and criticism to the status quo be called "prophets"?

7. How do those who claim to represent the people usurp the rights of the unrepresented and the underrepresented?

8. What are the causes of residential ghetto areas in the metropolis?

9. How can the plumb line of God's justice be set down beside discrimination in housing?

10. Is the fall of human beings in the city a natural event like the fall of a sparrow?

Chapter IV. The City of Man and the City of God

1. Of what significance is the fact that the first cities were created for divine purposes as burial places or sanctuaries rather than as fortresses or trade centers?

2. What is your understanding of the relation of the city of God to the city of man?

3. What difference has the coming of Christ made for the life of the metropolis?

4. What has been the effect on metropolitan areas of the changes brought by migration, automobiles, radio and television, labor-saving devices and automation?

5. Why have American cities failed to appreciate the magnitude of the task of social reconstruction facing them?

6. Do you agree that there is a "suburban" state of mind?

7. What factors do you feel are necessary in a metropolitan strategy?

8. Why can small actions or words often produce great changes, in spite of the forces of conformity and inertia?

9. Can youth be held responsible for "juvenile delinquency" or must the community bear its share of the blame?

10. What distinguishes the Christian hope from simple optimism?

Chapter V. What Can the Church Do?

1. What forces have contributed to Protestant churches' isolation from the urban power structure? What forces have been counteracting this trend?

2. In what ways can God be seen working "in spite of the churches and beyond them, as well as through them"?

3. What does it mean to call the church "the people of God," "the light of the world"?

4. What place do professional church workers have in the life of the church? What place do church members have?

5. Think about the ways in which your own church bears witness through worship; through teaching; through service. How can the members of a church be faithful to God in their daily life in the metropolitan area?

6. Why is it important that church members accept responsibility within the pyramids of power, especially in the field of politics?

7. Is it wrong for a local congregation to take a stand on a community issue as a congregation? What contribution can be made to the life of the church in a metropolitan area by denominational judicatories? by councils of churches?

8. What is the role of the Holy Spirit in the life of the metropolitan church?

052467